PUBLIC SPENDING AND DEMOCRACY
IN CLASSICAL ATHENS

Ashley and Peter Larkin Series in Greek and Roman Culture

PUBLIC SPENDING
AND DEMOCRACY IN
CLASSICAL ATHENS

DAVID M. PRITCHARD

UNIVERSITY OF TEXAS PRESS
Austin

First edition, 2015
First paperback printing, 2016

Requests for permission to reproduce material
from this work should be sent to:
Permissions
University of Texas Press
P.O. Box 7819
Austin, TX 78713-7819
http://utpress.utexas.edu/index.php/rp-form

♾ The paper used in this book meets the minimum
requirements of ANSI/NISO Z39.48–1992 (R1997)
(Permanence of Paper).

Library of Congress Cataloging-in-Publication Data
Pritchard, David, 1970–, author.
Public spending and democracy in Classical Athens /
David M. Pritchard. — First edition.
pages   cm — (Ashley and Peter Larkin series in
Greek and Roman culture)
Includes bibliographical references and index.

ISBN 978-0-292-77203-8 (cloth : alk. paper) —
ISBN 978-0-292-77204-5 (library e-book) —
ISBN 978-0-292-77205-2 (non-library e-book)
1. Finance, Public—Greece—Athens—History—To 1500.
2. Athens (Greece)—Appropriations and expenditures—
History—To 1500.   3. Democracy—Greece—Athens—
History—To 1500.   4. War and society—Greece—
Athens—History—To 1500.   5. War—Economic
aspects—Greece—Athens—History—To 1500.   I. Title.
II. Series: Ashley and Peter Larkin series in
Greek and Roman culture.
HJ217.P75   2015
336.3'909385—dc23
2014046224

ISBN 978-1-4773-1134-9, paperback
doi:10.7560/772038

CONTENTS

ILLUSTRATIONS

TABLES

ABBREVIATIONS

ANCIENT AUTHORS AND WORKS

Aesch.	Aeschylus
Ag.	*Agamemnon*
Eum.	*Eumenides*
Sept.	*Septem contra Thebas* (*Seven against Thebes*)
Aeschin.	Aeschines
Andoc.	Andocides
[Andoc.]	Pseudo-Andocides
Anth. Pal.	*Anthologia Palatina*
Antiph.	Antiphon
Ar.	Aristophanes
Ach.	*Acharnenses* (*Acharnians*)
Av.	*Aves* (*Birds*)
Eccl.	*Ecclesiazusae* (*Assemblywomen*)
Eq.	*Equites* (*Knights*)
Lys.	*Lysistrata*
Nub.	*Nubes* (*Clouds*)
Pax	*Pax* (*Peace*)
Plut.	*Plutus* (*Wealth*)
Thesm.	*Thesmophoriazusae* (*Women Celebrating the Festival of the Thesmophoria*)
Ran.	*Ranae* (*Frogs*)
Vesp.	*Vespae* (*Wasps*)
Arist.	Aristotle
Pol.	*Politica* (*Politics*)

Rh.	*Rhetorica* (*Rhetoric*)
[Arist.]	Pseudo-Aristotle
Ath. Pol.	*Athenaion Politeia* (*Constitution of the Athenians*)
Ath.	Athenaeus
Dem.	Demosthenes
[Dem.]	Pseudo-Demosthenes
Din.	Dinarchus
Diod. Sic.	Diodorus Siculus
Diog. Laert.	Diogenes Laertius
Eup.	Eupolis
Eur.	Euripides
Heracl.	*Heraclidae* (*Children of Heracles*)
Phoen.	*Phoenissae* (*Phoenician Women*)
Supp.	*Supplices* (*Suppliant Women*)
Tro.	*Troades* (*Trojan Women*)
Hdt.	Herodotus
Hell. Oxy.	*Hellenica Oxyrhynchia*
Hyp.	Hyperides
Isae.	Isaeus
Isoc.	Isocrates
Lycurg.	Lycurgus
Lys.	Lysias
Men.	Menander
Dys.	*Dyskolos* (*Bad-Tempered Man*)
Nep.	Nepos
Timoth.	*Timotheus*
Paus.	Pausanias
Pind.	Pindar
Isthm.	*Isthmian Odes*
Nem.	*Nemean Odes*
Ol.	*Olympian Odes*
Pyth.	*Pythian Odes*
Pl.	Plato
Grg.	*Gorgias*
Ion	*Ion*
Leg.	*Leges* (*Laws*)

Menex.	*Menexenus*
Phdr.	*Phaedrus*
Prt.	*Protagoras*
Resp.	*Respublica* (*Republic*)
Plut.	Plutarch
Arist.	*Aristeides*
De glor. Ath.	*De Gloria Atheniensium* (*On the Glory of Athens*)
Mor.	*Moralia*
Nic.	*Nicias*
Per.	*Pericles*
Quaest. Plat.	*Quaestiones Platonicae*
Them.	*Themistocles*
[Plut.]	Pseudo-Plutarch
Dec. Orat.	*Vitae decem oratorum*
Poll.	Pollux
Polyaen.	Polyaenus
Soph.	Sophocles
Aj.	*Ajax*
Thuc.	Thucydides
Xen.	Xenophon
An.	*Anabasis*
Eq. Mag.	*de Equitum Magistro* (*On the Cavalry Commander*)
Hell.	*Hellenica*
Mem.	*Memorabilia*
Oec.	*Oeconomicus*
Vect.	*De Vectigalibus* (*Ways and Means*)
[Xen.]	Pseudo-Xenophon
Ath. Pol.	*Athenaion Politeia* (*Constitution of the Athenians*)

EDITIONS AND EPIGRAPHICAL
COMPILATIONS OF ANCIENT SOURCES

Blass and Fuhr	F. Blass and K. Fuhr (ed. and comm.), *Andocides: Orationes*. Teubner, 1913.
Collard, Cropp, and Lee	C. Collard, M. Cropp, and K. H. Lee (eds. and trans.), *Euripides: Selected Fragmentary Plays, Volume 1*. Warminster, 1995.
FGrH	F. Jacoby (ed. and comm.), *Fragmente der griechischen Historiker*. Berlin, 1923–.
Gernet and Bizos	L. Gernet and M. Bizos (eds. and trans.), *Lysias: Discours: texte établi et traduit*. 2 volumes. Paris, 1924–1955.
Hell. Oxy.	*Hellenica Oxyrhynchia*
IG	*Inscriptiones Graecae*. Berlin, 1873–.
Jenkins	I. Jenkins, *The Parthenon Frieze*. London, 1994.
Kassel and Austin	R. Kassel and C. Austin (eds.), *Poetae Comici Graeci*. Berlin, 1983–2001.
ML	R. Meiggs and D. M. Lewis (ed. and comm.), *A Selection of Greek Historical Inscriptions to the End of the Fifth Century*. Oxford, 1969.
RO	P. J. Rhodes and R. Osborne (eds., comm., and trans.), *Greek Historical Inscriptions 404–323 BC*. Oxford, 2003.
Rose	V. Rose (ed.), *Aristotelis Qui Ferebantur Librorum Fragmenta*. Leipzig, 1886.
SEG	*Supplementum Epigraphicum Graecum*. 1923–.
Wehrli	F. Wehrli (ed. and comm.), *Die Schule des Aristoteles: Texte und Kommentare*. Basel, 1944–1959.

JOURNAL ABBREVIATIONS

ABSA	*Annual of the British School at Athens*
AC	*L'antiquité classique*
AD	*Archaiologikon Deltion*
AEph	*Archaiologike ephemeris*
AH	*Ancient History*
AHR	*American Historical Review*
AJAH	*American Journal of Ancient History*
AJPh	*American Journal of Philology*
AncW	*The Ancient World*
C&M	*Classica et mediaevalia*
ClAnt	*Classical Antiquity*
CPh	*Classical Philology*
CQ	*Classical Quarterly*
CR	*Classical Review*
G&R	*Greece and Rome*
GRBS	*Greek, Roman and Byzantine Studies*
JHS	*Journal of Hellenic Studies*
MDAI(A)	*Mitteilungen des Deutschen Archäologischen Instituts*
MediterrAnt	*Mediterraneo antico*
P&P	*Past and Present*
REG	*Revue des études grecques*
SO	*Symbolae Osloenses*
TAPhA	*Transactions and Proceedings of the American Philological Association*
ZPE	*Zeitschrift für Papyrologie und Epigraphik*

PREFACE

This book hopes to settle debates about public spending in classical Athens. It confirms the priorities that the Athenians set for their state. I began this book as a Postdoctoral Research Fellow at the University of Sydney. I completed it as a member of the University of Queensland's Cultural History Project. I wrote a lot of this book when I was a research fellow in the Institute for Advanced Studies in the Humanities at the University of Edinburgh. I am grateful to Douglas Cairns, who, along with his colleagues, supported my application for this fellowship and invited me to deliver the Charles Gordon Mackay Lectures in Greek for 2013. I am no less indebted to Josiah Ober, Kurt A. Raaflaub, and P. J. Rhodes, who read this book in its entirety and commented helpfully on it. Sincere thanks go to Peter Fawcett, Vincent Gabrielsen, and Hans van Wees for sharing with me their own scripts on Athenian public finance. Martin Bell and Philipp Ueffing of the University of Queensland kindly advised me on demographic modeling. I appreciated those who made suggestions on this book when I spoke about its findings in Athens, Brisbane, Christchurch, London, Melbourne, and Sydney. I thank the Nicholas Anthony Aroney Trust, which, for a fourth time, gave me a grant to complete a book. I acknowledge the editors who gave me permission to publish here material that first appeared in their journals. An early version of this book's argument was published as Pritchard 2012b. The section entitled "Magistrates" in Chapter 3 first appeared as Pritchard 2014. The section entitled "Public Spending on the Armed Forces in the 420s" in Chapter 4 is a revised version of Pritchard 2007b. I am indebted to Jim Burr of the University of Texas Press for quickly backing this book and ensuring its timely publication. I thank sincerely Nancy Moore for her outstanding copy editing. Calculating the public spending of classical Athens often seemed an impossibly difficult *ponos*. For her wonderful support as I attempted this toil, final thanks go to my wife, Dr. Jumana Bayeh. This book is dedicated entirely to Jumana.

Unless it is otherwise indicated, all of the book's translations are my own.

PUBLIC SPENDING AND DEMOCRACY
IN CLASSICAL ATHENS

ONE

PUBLIC-SPENDING DEBATES

This book calculates the public spending of classical Athens. In so doing it confirms the priorities that its citizens had for their state. The major public activities of the Athenian *dēmos* ("people") were the staging of religious festivals, the conducting of politics, and the waging of wars. There is hot debate about what was spent on these three public activities. Ancient historians cannot agree whether the *dēmos* spent more on festivals or wars. They debate how the classical Athenians paid for their democracy. These debates go back to the first modern book on Athenian public finance. In this book, August Böckh famously criticized the Athenians for wasting money on their festivals instead of building up their armed forces. His book argued too that their decision to pay themselves to run the democracy forced them to tax unjustly the subjects of their empire. Calculating what they spent on their public activities would settle both debates. Böckh lacked the evidence to do such calculations. Two centuries later, this is no longer the case. But in spite of our larger body of evidence we are still not able to compare costs over the classical period's full course. Such a comparison is only possible within a shorter period of eighty years.

Yet this book does more than settle two longstanding debates. In classical Athens the *dēmos* had full control over public spending. In the assembly they authorized the one-off activities of their *polis* ("city-state") and any changes to its recurring activities. Assemblygoers understood the financial consequences of their decisions. They knew how much a proposal that was put before them would cost and what proportion of public income it would use up. They had a good general knowledge of what the *polis* spent on its major activities. Consequently they could judge whether a proposal cost the same as what was normally spent on such things. This knowledge made it possible for the Athenians to change their pattern of spending and so what they spent on one class of activities relative to others. Such votes allowed the *dēmos* to spend more on what they saw as a priority and less on what was less of a priority. Over time the sums they spent on different public activities reflected the order of the priorities that they had set for their *polis*. By calculating these sums, I am able to confirm whether religious festivals, democratic politics, or military campaigns were the Athenian people's overriding priority.

FESTIVALS AND WARS

In his *Die Staatshaushaltung der Athener* (*The Public Economy of Athens*) of 1817 August Böckh (figure 1.1) criticized the classical Athenian *dēmos* for spending more on festivals than on wars.[1] By "squandering away the public revenue in shows and banquets at home," they caused their armed forces to be "in a continually declining state."[2] For Böckh this policy was "unjust and inexpedient, inasmuch as the continuance of it without oppressing the allies was impossible, and the State, being deprived of the means of self-defense in a most frivolous and unpardonable manner, was led on to certain destruction."[3] In support of his criticism, Böckh cited an assembly speech of 352/1 BC, in which Demosthenes unfavorably compared Athens' waging of war to its staging of festivals (4.35–37; cf. Diod. Sic. 13.94.1–2; Isoc. 7.52–53): "In matters pertaining to war and its preparations (*paraskeuēi*) everything is disordered (*atakta*), uncorrected, and indeterminate (*aorista*—36)."[4] Consequently all naval expeditions (*tous d'apostolous pantas*) are sent out too late to prevent Philip of Macedon taking city after city (35, 37). By contrast, the preparations for the City Dionysia and the Great Panathenaea are ordered (*tetaktai*) by law, guaranteeing that the sponsors of choruses and the teams know exactly

FIGURE 1.1.
August Böckh. Lithograph. Berlin, Porträtsammlung Berliner
Hochschullehrer, Humboldt-Universität zu Berlin, Inv. No. 7188.
© *UB der HU zu Berlin.*

what to do and "nothing remains unexamined and indeterminate (*aoriston* — 36).

For Demosthenes the result was that the two festivals took place on time, had greater crowds and paraphernalia (*paraskeuēn*) than any other, and used up more money than was spent even on a single naval expedition (*eis hēna tōn apostolōn*). Böckh suggested that "this weak point" was also recognized by Plutarch, who proposed in his *On the Glory of Athens*: "If the cost of the production of each drama were reckoned, the Athenian people would appear to have spent more on the production of *Bacchaes* and *Phoenician Women* and *Oedipuses* and the misfortunes of Medeas and Electras than they did on maintaining their empire and fighting for their liberty against the Persians."[5]

In his book's two volumes Böckh exhaustively canvassed the evidence that was then available on the scale and the expenses of the festivals of classical Athens and its armed forces.[6] The citizens of this *polis*, of course, inscribed many of their assembly decrees on stone and insisted that their magistrates do the same with financial accounts.[7] Böckh was the first to realize fully the importance of such evidence for Ancient History.[8] Consequently more than a quarter of *The Public Economy of Athens* is taken up by his discussion of various inscriptions. This realization also prompted Böckh as he was writing his book to begin the first collection of Greek inscriptions.[9] His *Corpus Inscriptionum Graecarum* proved to be a much larger task than he anticipated, and so it was completed by others only half a century later. Since its completion, several hundreds of new stelae from classical Attica have been discovered.[10] In spite of his exhaustiveness, Böckh thus saw only a fraction of the inscriptions we have today.

Böckh had no access either to the *Constitution of the Athenians*, which ancient writers attributed to Aristotle.[11] In 1891 the British Museum caused a worldwide sensation when it announced its discovery of this lost treatise on four rolls of papyrus from Egypt.[12] The first half of this work charts Athenian constitutional changes to 404/3, while its second half describes the democracy as it was in the 320s.[13] Today's majority view is that its author was not Aristotle but one of his students in his school in Athens.[14] Nevertheless, this treatise enormously expanded our knowledge of this state's institutions. When he wrote *The Public Economy of Athens*, Böckh simply lacked the evidence to calculate how much the classical Athenians spent on their major public activities.[15] Two centuries after his book, this is no longer the case. This book is thus able to estimate and to compare the costs of these three public activities. In doing so, it tests Böckh's harsh criticisms of Athenian public spending and the literary evidence that he cited in support of them.

The task of costing total spending on Athenian festivals is made easier by recent studies of the cost of the City Dionysia.[16] They have been spawned by the shift of scholarly focus towards the "social context" of Greek theater during the last generation.[17] The City Dionysia and the Great Panathenaea were by far the largest festivals of the Athenian *polis* (e.g., Ar. *Pax* 416–420).[18] Costing either festival thus sheds light on a significant proportion of the full cost of its festival program. The first to do so carefully for the City Dionysia were Eric Csapo and William Slater, who concluded, in *The Context of Ancient Drama*, that Athens of the later fifth century contributed 6 talents to the City Dionysia, while its chorus sponsors spent 18 talents 5,800 drachmas of their own money.[19] The second of their figures was initially supported by Peter Wilson, whose independent calculations, in *The Athenian Institution of the Khoregia: The Chorus, the City and the Stage*, yielded a figure "just short of a massive 18 talents for five days' choral performance."[20] The talent (t.) was the largest weight of the silver currency of classical Athens. It was the equivalent of about 26 kilograms. The smallest weight was the obol (ob.), while the most commonly used intermediate weight was the drachma (dr.). There were 6 ob. in 1 dr. and 6,000 dr. in 1 t.

Subsequently, in 2008, Wilson completed a new study of this question as part of the project that he and Csapo codirected on the social and economic history of ancient Greek drama.[21] His study uses a vast array of often overlooked evidence from fifth- and fourth-century Attica and comparative material from elsewhere to estimate how much this festival cost around 415. His final figure for public spending on the pay of the poets and musicians, the equipment, and the beasts for sacrifice is 13 t. 1,300 dr., while the private outlay of the chorus sponsors and the supervisors of the procession adds up to 15 t. 3,900 dr.[22] Of these costings, this later attempt by Wilson is clearly the most thorough and reliable. Therefore, his grand total of 28 t. 5,200 dr. for the City Dionysia will be incorporated into this book's calculations.

These costings have renewed the early confidence in Böckh's view of what classical Athens spent on its festivals and the literary evidence that he cited as support for it.[23] For example, Csapo and Slater believe the comment of Plutarch "though exaggerated, is not wildly so."[24] Citing their figures, Lisa Kallet suggests that the two passages "reflect a popular perception of heavy expenditure on festivals," which—she believes—is factually correct, while Wilson concludes that "ancient claims about Athenian expenditure on their theatre are fully justified."[25] Such conclusions bolster the long-held view that religion was the topmost priority of the Greek *polis* in classical times.[26] Some who hold this view even argue that the appeasing of the gods was the highest priority of the Athenian *dēmos*.[27] Hugh Bowden for one concludes that "Athenian democracy was above all a system for establishing and reinforcing the will of the gods."[28] For Bowden, the enormous sums that it spent on festivals bears this out.[29]

These ancient historians call into question the consensus of those who work on Athenian wars. Military historians hold the view that the military spending of classical Athens far exceeded what it spent on all of its other activities combined.[30] Yet with only a handful of exceptions, they have shied away from estimating war's full financial cost, because of its great variability between the centuries and from year to year.[31] Instead they aim for only a general sense of the scale of military spending by detailing the known costs of sieges, the known recurring spending on particular corps, or their own calculations of the cost of an "average" armada.[32] It is not possible to adjudicate this debate as it currently stands: those renewing Böckh's negative view have costed only part of the city's festival program, while the opposing view of military historians is based on only some of war's costs. Consequently this book estimates the full cost of both activities so that this public-spending debate can be settled.

DEMOCRACY

The classical Athenians also spent a lot of public funds on their system of government. Largely this was due to the introduction of *misthophoria* ("receipt of pay") for political participation.[33] Pericles backed the giving of *misthos* ("pay") to jurors in the 450s.[34] Pay for councilors and magistrates followed probably in the 440s or the 430s. These first forms of state pay were introduced at a time when the democracy had become much busier than ever before. By the mid-fifth century most legal cases were judged by hundreds of jurors.[35] Incessant wars and the administration of the Delian League had forced the council of five hundred and the assembly to meet more frequently.[36] With a larger population and more festivals, hundreds of new magistracies had been created.

The vast majority of Athenians were of course poor. What they had in common was a lack of *skholē* ("leisure").[37] Wealth relieved the wealthy of the need of working and hence gave them this leisure (e.g., Ar. *Plut.* 281, *Vesp.* 552–557; Men. *Dys.* 293–295). But the poor had to work for a living (e.g., Ar. *Pax* 632, *Vesp.* 611, *Plut.* 281; Lys. 24.16).[38] Consequently they could have helped to transact this public business only if they were compensated for lost earnings. Thus, the most likely reason for this new *misthophoria* was that it ensured that there would be enough citizens to run the expanding democracy.[39] In Aristotle's words, "receiving *misthos*" made the poor "able to have *skholē*" for political participation (*Pol.* 1293a1–10).[40] This subsidization of the poor's participation in politics clearly was an innovation of fifth-century Athens, as no evidence exists of it elsewhere until the next century.[41]

The public support of the poor's participation in politics went beyond these payments. Soon after the democracy's second restoration in 404/3, the Athenians introduced pay for assemblygoers. This *misthos* was subsequently raised several times. By the 330s it had become the costliest of the democracy's recurring costs. Classical Athens made it possible for a larger number of its poor citizens to serve as magistrates by giving every board of them a *hupogrammateus* or undersecretary. Certainly many Athenians as boys had attended the classes of a *grammatistēs* or letter teacher.[42] But some left school before they had learned to read and to write confidently, as their families required them to help keep farms or businesses going (e.g., Dem. 18.256–267; Isoc. 7.43–45; Lys. 20.11–12).[43] In the absence of clerical staff, such citizens would have simply not volunteered to be magistrates. They would have been too daunted at the prospect of keeping accounts and being quizzed on them later at their public audit. This availability of undersecretaries meant that Athenian magistrates were not required to be literate.[44] The *dēmos* also provided public slaves to assist magistrates in the carrying out of their duties and from the 330s began awarding gold crowns to officials whose service they judged to have been exemplary. We can thus see that the subsidization of nonelite participation in politics consisted of more than *misthos*: it also included assistance for the functionally illiterate, the provision of slave assistants, and a costly incentives scheme.

Certainly Böckh was no less critical of what the classical Athenians spent on political participation.[45] As a political conservative who preferred monarchy to democracy, he abhorred the support for popular government that the French Revolution had created.[46] Böckh followed William Mitford in seeing classical Athens as an example of democracy's dangers, which discredited contemporary support for it.[47] On *misthos* for politics Böckh opined: "Unless the governing power is to fall into the hands of the mob, the people should receive no pecuniary compensation for their share in government."[48] He added: "It is a condition requisite for good government that all who wish to partake in the ruling power should support themselves upon their property."[49] He considered pay for political participation to be "an expense which it is impossible to pay by incomes justly raised."[50] For Böckh the Athenians paid for it by exploiting their allies.[51]

In the century that followed the publication of *The Public Economy of Athens*, many democracies were introduced. In England of the later nineteenth century, George Grote corrected the generally negative view of classical Athens so that this ancient democracy could serve as support for extending the right to vote.[52] Thus, ancient historians came to judge Athens more positively than Böckh. In spite of this, many persisted with his view that pay for political participation was provided by imperial tribute.[53] It remained a common charge against Athenian democracy that it was "parasitic on the empire."[54]

A. H. M. Jones challenged this charge sixty years ago.[55] His "very simple answer" was that the democracy continued in the fourth century when the *arkhē* or empire had been lost.[56] With *misthos* for assemblygoers, it even managed to introduce "a new and important source of pay." Jones concluded: "That Athens profited financially from her empire is of course true. But these profits were not necessary to keep the democracy working."[57] Twenty years later Jones himself was challenged by Sir Moses Finley.[58] Finley conceded that the democracy kept going. This he put down to a resilience of institutions.[59] Although it was "difficult" for fourth-century Athenians "to provide the necessary financial underpinnings," the democracy "was so deeply entrenched that no one dared to attempt to replace it." But Finley reasserted Böckh's view of the imperial income: without it, fifth-century Athens could never have afforded to subsidize the poor's involvement in politics.[60] Because this nonelite participation drove the democracy's final institutional development, Finley concluded that "the empire" really was "a necessary condition for the Athenian type of democracy."[61] Ancient historians have taken different sides in this debate: for example, Mogens Herman Hansen, Lisa Kallet, and Josiah Ober have rejected Finley's conclusion, while Edmund Burke, Loren Samons, and Robert Sinclair have supported it.[62]

Calculating what the democracy cost would go a long way to settling this debate, and so the small part that running costs have played in it is a surprise. Jones judged it "hardly worthwhile to go into the financial figures" but did so nonetheless.[63] Thus, he calculated the annual cost of magistrates at 21 t. in the 330s.[64] Pay for councilors was "considerably less" than 26 t. per year. For Jones *misthos* for assemblygoers "cannot be calculated as we do not know how large the quorum was." But he did put jury pay under 150 t. in the 420s. At the outbreak of the Peloponnesian War in 432/1 the annual income that Athens raised at home was 400 t.[65] This led Jones to conclude: "Since other peace-time expenditure was minimal, pay was thus amply covered by internal income in this period."[66] The problems in this costing were clear. Jones mixed up costs from different centuries and made some vague estimates. He simply guessed what other nonmilitary spending had been.[67]

Those who joined this debate chose not to address these problems. They relied much less on figures than Jones did. Finley used none whatsoever in his reassertion of Böckh's view. To his credit, Hansen worked out how large the assembly's quorum was and so was able to establish the cost of assembly pay.[68] This he put at about 50 t. in the 330s.[69] But this estimate of only one running cost emboldened him to go further than Jones. For Hansen, it not only refuted Finley's conclusion that tribute made the fifth-century democracy possible. It also showed how the fourth-century democracy "must have been a much more costly institution than the imperialistic democracy led by Pericles."[70] Sinclair's use of figures was no sounder. He estimated the yearly cost of jury pay at 22 t. in the 450s, when internal revenue may have been 300 t.[71] But Sinclair cautioned that "this revenue had to meet other needs of the Athenian *polis*," and so "the introduction of state pay would have been difficult without rising revenue or heavier imposts on the wealthy." For Sinclair, tribute made it possible to introduce this *misthophoria* without taxing wealthy citizens more. Because heavier taxation would have incurred their opposition, he concluded that the *arkhē* made it easier to subsidize the poor's involvement in politics. The problems here were the same as in earlier costings. Sinclair made no attempt to estimate public spending on other public activities, while a conclusion about the democracy's overall cost was based on only one of its fixed operating costs.

Estimating the full cost of Athenian democracy is made considerably easier by Hansen's work. He may not have settled the Böckh-Jones debate, but he has significantly advanced our understanding of Athenian institutions. More than any other ancient historian, Hansen has quantified their activity and the participation of Athenians in them. In due course this quantification has allowed him to make the most reliable estimate of the democracy's total cost. Hansen calculates that it cost between 92 and 112 t. per year in the 330s.[72] This estimate has been widely accepted.[73] Hansen's focus on the later fourth century is understandable. The survival of the *Constitution of the Athenians* by Aristotle's pupil and many public speeches make it the best documented period for the history of Athenian institutions. But this focus does not help us to settle this public-spending debate. To do so we need to know how much government cost during the Athenian empire. The administration of this *arkhē* forced Athens to create many more magistracies and to hear a lot more legal cases. The result is that we cannot assume that the democracy in the age of Pericles cost the same as it would a century later.

A focus on the 330s also rules out a comparison between the costs of the three major public activities. We will see that such a comparison is possible only if we estimate the democracy's running costs in the 420s and the 370s.[74] In doing so we must often work backwards from the better-documented 330s, and so in this book I also calculate these costs in the 330s. This also allows us to fix the problems in Hansen's calculation. The most serious of them is that he argues that magistrates were not paid in the fourth century. His argument was always contentious and appears to be wrong. Including the *misthos* of magistrates significantly raises the cost of the government in the 370s and the 330s. Hansen too shies away from costing their undersecretaries and public slaves and greatly overestimates the cost of their incentives scheme.

THE PERIOD OF EIGHTY YEARS
FOR COMPARING COSTS

The comparing of the costs of the three major activities of classical Athens is possible only in the period from 430 to 350. Before the Peloponnesian War the surviving evidence is simply too limited to allow for reliable estimates of the costs of the city's festivals, politics, and wars. For the eighty years that this book covers, spending on state-sponsored festivals was remarkably stable. Most of the democracy's new festivals were introduced before 460, the number of festival liturgies remained relatively steady during the Peloponnesian War, the final defeat in this war had no discernible impact on what wealthy citizens spent on these public services, and "there is little evidence of the Athenians intervening with the way in which major festivals were celebrated in the first half of the fourth century."[75] This stability enables the generation of cost estimates of Athenian festivals that hold true from 430 to 350 on the basis of the surviving evidence from across this period. Indeed such estimates would not be possible without this aggregating of data, because what testimonia we have for Athenian religious celebrations are simply too thin and chronologically scattered to support costings of them in a smaller timeframe of, for example, a decade or a quarter of a century.

Spending on the armed forces varied greatly between 430 and 350. The loss of one half or more of the citizen population during the Peloponnesian War and the collapse of the tribute-bearing *arkhē* at its close significantly reduced the scale of war that Athens could wage in the fourth century.[76] This necessitates separate costings of the armed forces in the later fifth century and in the first half of the next century. For the first of these estimates we are unable to go back further than the late 430s. We may know that the siege of Samos of 441/0 to 440/39 cost Athens 1,276 t. (Isoc. 15.111; Nep. *Timoth.* 1; *IG* i³ 363), but, before 433/2, we lack figures for total military spending in any year or period and even for the basic parameters of known campaigns, which would allow us, at least, to build up an estimate of spending campaign by campaign.

This lack of firm evidence for basic parameters scuttles the attempt of Ron Unz to calculate how much Athens spent on war between 478/7 and 433/2, which he estimated at 13,000 t. or close to an average of 300 t. per year.[77] In the absence of hard information, his calculations assume that fleets were away for the full sailing season of eight months and that their participants were each paid only 3 ob. per day.[78] Neither assumption is secure.[79] A more recent study of the better-documented years of 433/2 to 426/5 suggests that there was no standard length of time for Athenian expeditions in the later fifth century, with fleets away from only a few months to many months more than the regular sailing season.[80] The case may now be closed that the daily pay for Athenian sailors and hoplites was 1 dr. between 433/2 and 412/1 (e.g., Thuc. 3.17.4, 6.8.1, 6.31.3, 7.27.1–2).[81] But we still do not know when exactly hoplites began to be paid and when 1 dr. became the standard daily rate.[82]

The great interest that the new genre of historiography took in the Peloponnesian War and the large number of literary and epigraphical sources surviving from it mean that the situation is different from the late 430s. We have consistently detailed information about the Peloponnesian War's campaigns and reliable figures for public income at its outbreak. For its first phase, which is called the Archidamian War, we also have surviving inscriptions that record the annual tribute that the subject cities of the *arkhē* paid the Athenians and the sacred monies that they borrowed to cover their war effort. Military historians may have shied away from costing the Peloponnesian War or any other conflict for that matter. But these figures for public income and sacred loans, when they are carefully added up, furnish annual totals of public spending on the armed forces in the 420s.[83]

For the first fifty years of the next century the lack of more than a few figures for public finances stops us from using the same method for costing Athenian warmaking after the Peloponnesian War. Thus, the only other method that is available is the identifying of individual expenses and the estimating of each one on the basis of surviving evidence and arguments from probability. The sum of these calculations yields an estimate of the full cost of the armed forces that is the most reliable possible without detailed information on public finances. This tedious exercise is made easier if individual expenses are grouped according to the basic cost classes of modern economics: capital costs, fixed operating costs, and variable operating costs.[84] Into the first cost class go what the Athenians spent on the "capital" of war, namely, ships, dockyards, fortifications, war horses, weapons, and armor. The second covers the expenses that Athens and its trierarchs paid to keep the armed forces going regardless of whether or not they were formally at war. The final cost class includes the costs of the expeditions and the campaigns that Athens chose to launch in any particular year.

From the early 370s to the later 450s enough evidence survives to estimate reliably the first two of these cost classes. The same cannot be said for variable operating costs. The *Hellenica* of Xenophon, which is our major source for this period, ostensibly narrated Greek foreign affairs from the exact point in 411/0 at which Thucydides abruptly stopped to the battle of Mantinea in 363/2. But this author, who lived away from Athens for most of his life, notoriously failed to cover Athenian campaigns in the northern Aegean, which was the major theater of Athenian military operations in the 360s. For this decade and the next we must rely then on the extant speeches of Athenian litigants and politicians, who mentioned only those campaigns that were relevant to their briefs and, when they did, did not normally canvass any of their basic parameters.[85] These sources thus do not allow us to estimate reliably the variable operating costs of any one year.[86]

Fortunately Xenophon did pay close attention to the campaigns of the 370s, which were waged against his beloved Spartans. With its "great density of numerous and varied sources," this decade is "better known" than the others of the fourth century and is the only one for which we can reliably estimate variable operating costs year by year.[87] Thus, for the fourth century's first fifty years, this major activity can be reliably costed only in the 370s. This book estimates both the full cost of the Athenian armed forces in the 420s and the 370s and the full cost of Athenian festivals that is valid for both decades. Consequently we must also cost the democracy during the same two decades so that a cost comparison of the three major public activities of classical Athens is possible.

The Athenians made significant changes to the financing of their armed forces and their festivals after 350. In the so-called Social War of 357 to 355 Athens had more ships at sea than at any time since the Peloponnesian War (Diod. Sic. 16.12).[88] The enormous cost of this conflict and the loss of the city's largest allies in the final defeat caused many sources of public income to dry up (Xen. *Vect.* 5.12), the annual income of the city to plunge to 130 t. (Dem. 10.37), and the economy as a whole to contract (Isoc. 8.19–21).[89] After some years of debates in public and in private about how best to address this financial crisis (e.g., Dem. 13.1–5), the *dēmos* finally passed, by 349/8 at the latest, the reforms that Eubulus and others had developed (Dem. 1.19–20, 3.11–13).

These reforms redirected any surplus of the city's annual public income into a new *theōrikon* or festival fund, whose initial purpose was to provide citizens with the necessary cash to buy entrance to the city's dramatic contests.[90] In spite of the confusion in ancient sources about this fund, Eberhard Ruschenbusch has established that Eubulus' introduction of this payment (also known as the *theōrikon*) around 350 "must no longer be called into question."[91] In the wake of the defeat, Athens began recovering remarkably quickly. By 353/2 the scale of its naval expeditions had returned to the level of the 360s.[92] In the late 340s its annual income had bounced back to 400 t. (Dem. 10.38), and, once the *theōrikon* had built up sufficiently, Eubulus and the fund's other managers introduced participation subsidies for other city-based festivals and paid directly for shipbuilding and other capital costs of war (e.g., Aeschin. 3.25–26; Din. 1.96). Yet the reforms of Eubulus significantly changed the state's financing of the armed forces. Consequently we cannot assume that their capital costs and fixed operating costs, which can be reliably estimated from the early 370s to the later 350s, stayed the same after 349/8.

These reforms also inaugurated ever-increasing spending by the *dēmos* and private citizens on state-sponsored festivals. For want of evidence, the *theōrika* payments cannot be reliably costed,[93] but they must have added up to a significant total for Demades to have called them the "cement of the democracy" (Plut. *Quaest. Plat.* 1011b). After their comprehensive defeat at the battle of Chaeronea in 338/7, the Athenian *dēmos* voted for the proposals of Lycurgus and other leading citizens for expanding their program of festivals.[94] New festivals and public sacrifices were introduced, existing festivals picked up new *agōnes* ("contests") and more sumptuous celebrations every four years, and wealthy priests began spending more out of their own pockets.[95] In light of these significant changes, a comparison of the costs of the three major activities after 350 would require new costings of public spending on festivals and the armed forces. The lacunose state of the evidence in this period and the difficulty of including pre-350 testimonia cast doubt on the feasibility of such estimates. They are certainly beyond this book's scope.

THE DEMOCRATIC CONTROL
OF PUBLIC SPENDING

In classical Athens the *dēmos* had full control over public spending. In the assembly they authorized the extraordinary activities of their city and the changes to its recurring activities. They were well informed of the financial implications of their votes. The council of five hundred members monitored the revenues and the expenses of the *polis* closely. Hence this democratic council could advise them whether extra funds had to be raised for what they had previously voted for. In the assembly's debates the politician who supported a proposal had to cost it accurately and to show how this cost related to the *polis*'s fiscal position. If a rival convinced assemblygoers that his proposal was unaffordable he also had to advise how its cost could be reduced or where new income or cash reserves could be found to pay for it. In voting for such a proposal, assemblygoers were thus making a decision not only on its merit but also on the proportion of public income that should be devoted to it.

Their constant adjudicating of such debates developed their general knowledge of what was spent on their three major public activities. Consequently the *dēmos* could judge whether a proposal cost the same as what was normally spent on such things. This made it easier for them to change their pattern of spending and hence what they spent on one class of activities relative to others. Over time such votes allowed assemblygoers to spend more on what they saw a priority and less on what they saw as less of a priority. As the classical period progressed, they became much better too at setting budgets for future spending. Without doubt, the sums that the Athenian *dēmos* spent on their public activities reflected clearly the order of the priorities they had for their *polis*.

By the 430s the Athenian *dēmos* entirely controlled the financing of festivals. Consequently a *heortē* ("festival") could be expanded or a new one added to the state's program only by an assembly decree (e.g., *IG* i³ 82.25–30; ii² 1672.261).[96] The Athenians had long appointed *hieropoioi* ("doers of sacred things") and other magistrates to manage their festivals alongside the cult personnel who had traditionally done so (e.g., *IG* i³ 82.19–25).[97] The *dēmos* supervised closely how much was spent on each *heortē*.[98] They regularly set a festival's budget in whole or part (e.g., RO 81.B.10–25, 27–31). The earliest surviving example of such budgeting is a decree of the 460s concerning the Eleusinian Mysteries (*IG* i³ 6).[99] In it the *dēmos* set the fees that their priests and priestesses could charge initiates (*IG* i³ 6.C5–31). They set too how much of the cult's funds could be spent on the Mysteries (C14–20). When the *dēmos* judged that a deity did not have enough money for his or her worship, they often introduced a new tax on those who apparently benefited the most from his or her *kharis* ("gratitude"): shipowners, for example, were made to pay Poseidon and other maritime gods landing taxes (e.g., *IG* i³ 8.15–25), while the soldiers who used Apollo's athletics field for musters on the eve of campaigns paid him a poll tax (138.1–8).[100]

The Athenians manifestly saw the adequate funding of their festivals as essential (e.g., Dem. 24.26–28; RO 81.A.5–7).[101] But once a *heortē* had been paid for, they claimed the right to spend on secular purposes the sacred funds that remained.[102] This claim is evident too in the early decree on the Mysteries. It ordered the cult's *hieropoioi* to move Demeter and Persephone's funds to Athens (*IG* i³ 6.C36–38). Lines 32 to 36 state: "The Athenians will be permitted to use the sacred money of the fees for whatever they wish just as they do with Athena's money on the Acropolis."

In the 430s the *dēmos* came to realize fully the value of such money for war and so reorganized the sacred treasuries in which it lay in order that it could be spent more easily on military campaigns (e.g., Thuc. 2.13.2–3; *IG* i³ 78.40–44; cf. Dem. 22.69–78).[103] In a decree of 432/1 or slightly later, they created a new board of five *epistatai* ("supervisors") to take over responsibility for Demeter and Persephone's funds on the Acropolis (*IG* i³ 32.9–11).[104] This decree ordered the collection of all debts that were owed to the Two Goddesses and an audit of what their worship cost (14–30). Earlier, in 434/3, the *dēmos* passed a decree that consolidated the funds of their other deities — excepting Athena's — into one sacred treasury on the Acropolis (*IG* i³ 52).[105] It created a board of *tamiai* ("treasurers") to administer this new sacred treasury (*IG* i³ 52.A13–15). Their first duty was to calculate how much they had by counting or, in the case of uncoined bullion, weighing what had been collected from Attica's sanctuaries (A22–25). For each year that followed, the *tamiai* were ordered to publish on stone the yearly income of these other gods, what had been spent on their worship, and what cash was left over (A25–27; cf. *IG* i³ 383). It was this reorganization of sacred treasuries in the lead up to the Peloponnesian War that enabled Pericles to tell the *dēmos* how much money they had to spend on it (Thuc. 2.13.3–6). This war's first decade used up these cash reserves almost entirely (*IG* i³ 369).[106]

The Athenian *dēmos* had as much control over the funding of the armed forces as they had over religious expenses. From the later fifth century they likewise authorized what would be spent on war's capital costs, fixed operating costs, and variable operating costs. Whether warships would be built and, if so, how many consequently came down to their vote (e.g., [Arist.] *Ath. Pol.* 46.1; Thuc. 8.1.3; Xen. *Hell.* 5.4.34–35).[107] Assembly decrees were also required for spending on the dockyards and other military capital (e.g., *IG* i³ 52.A30–32). Likewise the *dēmos* set the *misthos* of the cavalry corps (e.g., Lys. fr. IV.73–70 Gernet and Bizos), which was the army's greatest recurring cost.[108]

The expedition that Athens sent to Sicily in 416/5 illustrates how assemblygoers sought to control the cost of each campaign. With this expedition they may have given their generals the power to work out its requirements (Thuc. 6.26.1), but they still passed a decree on its size and budget (*IG* i³ 93.7, 12–13, 47–49; Thuc.

6.43.1).[109] As this expedition went from bad to worse, repeated votes were taken on committing extra resources (Thuc. 6.94.4, 7.16.2). In approving a campaign the Athenian people sometimes stipulated which funds should be tapped for it (e.g., *IG* i³ 93.10–17). In 407/6, for instance, a new fleet had to be raised quickly to rescue Conon's warships, which the Spartans had trapped in Mytilene's harbor (Xen. *Hell.* 1.6.15–24). To pay for it, the *dēmos* voted to coin the last of the bullion—including Athena's statues—in the sacred treasuries (e.g., Hellanicus *FGrH* 323aF26).[110]

Ancient writers made the leading politicians of classical Athens responsible for introducing or increasing *misthos* for different types of political participation: Pericles, they wrote, introduced jury pay and Cleon raised it, while assembly pay was introduced by Agyrrhius and raised by Heraclides and Agyrrhius again (see "Festivals and Wars," above). These payments would have quite significantly affected public finance and so would have required the assembly's approval. Pericles and other politicians were no doubt remembered for pushing through the decree or the law that authorized each change to the *misthophoria* for politics.

The Athenian *dēmos* may have controlled public spending, but the day-to-day oversight of it fell to their council of five hundred.[111] In his description of the Athenian constitution, Aristotle's pupil explains how this council "administers together with the other magistrates most financial matters" ([Arist.] *Ath. Pol.* 47.1).[112] In the 320s, when he wrote, the *boulē* ("council") oversaw both income and expenditure. Athena's *tamiai* thus took over the money from their predecessors in the council's presence (47.1; cf. 44.1). In classical Athens it was the *pōlētai* ("sellers") who auctioned, among other items, the leases of public lands and silver mines, the contracts for tax collecting, and the property of defendants that the lawcourts had confiscated (e.g., 47.2; *IG* i³ 84.14–18).[113] In the later fourth century these auctions were conducted before the *boulē*, which apparently chose the winning bids ([Arist.] *Ath. Pol.* 47.2).[114] The council also held the records of the installments that the auction winners had to pay (47.5). Installments were consequently paid to the *apodektai* ("receivers"), who were chiefly responsible for collecting the city's income, in the *bouleutērion* or council chamber (48.1).[115] The *boulē* of the 320s, finally, ensured that the revenue so raised was allocated to the magistrates in charge of the funds for different public activities and only spent on what the *dēmos* had authorized (45.2, 48.2-3).

This financial oversight by the democratic council went back to the fifth century. The *hieropoioi*, for example, who managed the treasury of the Two Goddesses from the 460s and the *epistatai* who replaced them in the 430s worked under its supervision (*IG* i³ 32.14-15, 27-29; i³ 78.40-42; cf. [Xen.] *Ath. Pol.* 3.2). The *boulē* supervised too the treasurers of the other gods (*IG* i³ 52.A9-12). Before this last board was created, the council even appointed some of its own members as the treasurers of various gods (82.19-25, 138.9-12).[116] In the fifth century the *pōlētai* similarly took bids from prospective tax collectors before the *boulē* (Andoc. 1.134). By the 430s the council worked closely with the *apodektai* and the *hellēnotamiai* ("treasurers of Greece"), who administered the imperial treasury (e.g., *IG* i³ 52.A6-7, 9-12).[117] At this time the *kōlakretai* ("ham collectors") were "the principal spending officers of the Athenian state" and usually drew their funds from the city's secular treasury.[118] The council probably supervised this financial board as well.[119] The empire's subjects handed over their annual tribute in the Athenian *bouleutērion* ([Xen.] *Ath. Pol.* 3.2; *IG* i³ 34.5-11, 16-18). Likewise the *boulē* of the 420s made sure that magistrates did not misappropriate public funds (e.g., Antiph. 6.12, 35, 45, 49).

The council of five hundred met on no less than 275 days per year.[120] Public finance was apparently discussed in almost all of its meetings. In his *Constitution of the Athenians* Pseudo-Xenophon made "provision of money" second only to "the war" in his list of the matters on which the *boulē* invariably deliberated (3.2). In particular it was responsible for making sure that there was always enough income to cover expenditure (e.g., Ar. *Eq.* 773-776; Lys. 30.22). What allowed it to fulfill this responsibility was its supervision of the state's treasurers and other financial magistrates.[121] Each of these boards may have managed an important aspect of public finance. But the *bouleutai* ("councilors") oversaw all aspects and so could form a clear picture of the city's fiscal position. P. J. Rhodes writes: "Only the *boulē* had access to the information which would show whether the city could afford some new charge on its resources, and this must have been the reason for the *boulē's* financial predominance."[122]

In the democracy of classical Athens the council drafted the *probouleumata* ("preliminary proposals") that the assembly debated and voted on (e.g., [Arist.] *Ath. Pol.* 44.4, 45.4).[123] The *dēmos* could accept, modify, or reject such a proposal, but it could not consider an issue that was not covered by a *probouleuma*. This meant that if *bouleutai* were concerned about a funding shortfall, they could bring it to the people's attention and propose a way to meet it.[124] With the decree of 425/4, which trebled the *phoros* ("tribute"), they did just this (*IG* i³ 71). This decree put the *boulē* at the center of a rigorous new process for assessing the higher *phoros* that each of the empire's cities had to pay (e.g., *IG* i³ 71.8–9, 17–20). The council worked out this process itself (51). It justified this change on the grounds that the tribute, which was paying for the Peloponnesian War (46–50), "had become too little" (16–17). Hence the setting of the assembly's agenda by the *boulē* guaranteed that its knowledge of the city's total income and expenditure fed into the assembly's debates about public spending.

Athenian politicians also required a good knowledge of public finance.[125] Aristotle and Xenophon listed the five most important items of public business on which they had to be capable of speaking (Arist. *Rh.* 1.4.7–13; Xen. *Mem.* 3.6.1–14). In each of their lists, public finance was the topmost item. They also agreed on "the facts and figures related to public spending and revenue" that "a diligent would-be leader would have at his fingertips."[126] The overarching goal that a politician should have was to make the city richer (Arist. *Rh.* 1.4.8; Xen. *Mem.* 3.6.4–6). This required him to know its *prosodoi* ("incomes") and the total to which they came. He should be capable of suggesting new *prosodoi* and ways of increasing underperforming ones. For these fourth-century writers a competent politician knew too "all of the city's *dapanai* or expenses" (Arist. *Rh.* 1.4.8; cf. Xen. *Mem.* 3.6.6). As part of his effort to enrich it, he could tell the *dēmos* which of them were unnecessary and so dispensable and how the cost of others could be reduced.

The requirement for politicians to have such detailed knowledge indicates that they also played an important role in the assembly's public-spending debates. Certainly the *boulē* was primarily responsible for aggregating the disparate data on Athens' fiscal position,[127] but it was the public speakers who communicated this financial information to the *dēmos* and argued the pros and cons of each proposal. Therefore, if a politician wanted to support a *probouleuma*—or to propose a modified version of it—he needed to be capable of both costing it accurately and relating this *dapanē* to total income and spending. If a rival politician branded it as unaffordable, the politician would have to tell assemblygoers how its cost could be reduced or where a new *prosodos* could be found to pay for it.

This financial expertise on the part of politicians demonstrably went back to the 430s. Pericles for one told the assembly the cash reserves and the otherwise uncommitted public income that Athens could spend on the looming war with Sparta (Thuc. 2.13.3–5; cf. Plut. *Per.* 14.2). The politicians who followed him sought to win over the *dēmos* by producing "very much more money in the public treasury" (Ar. *Eq.* 773–776).[128] Indeed the tallying of the city's *prosodoi* and the relating of this tally to a *dapanē* had become so commonplace that such a calculation made it into contemporary comedies (e.g., *Vesp.* 655–663, 701–711).[129] In the wake, finally, of the Sicilian Expedition's destruction, a politician convinced the *dēmos* to replace the *phoros* with a tax on the empire's trade on the grounds that it would produce more income (Thuc. 7.28.4).[130]

The Athenian *dēmos* would appear then to have been well informed of the financial implications of their decisions.[131] When they voted, for example, to create a festival, to start a war, or to extend pay for political participation, they had a good idea what it would cost. Their politicians had told them which *prosodos* could be used or whether it required a new *prosodos* or the tapping of cash reserves. In voting on a proposal, assemblygoers were deciding too what portion of the city's income the proposal should use up. In constantly adjudicating public-spending debates, the *dēmos* consolidated their general knowledge of what Athens spent on its different activities.[132] The result was that assemblygoers sensed if a proposal would cost the same as what they normally spent on such things. This made it easier for them to change their normal spending pattern and so what they spent on one class of public activities relative to others. Over time such votes allowed the *dēmos* to spend more on what they saw as a priority and less on what they saw as less of a priority.

In general, democratic institutions serve as the "transmission belts" of such priorities: they translate the majority's preferences into public policies.[133] Two features of representative democracy impede this process.[134] The first is that in most modern democracies, citizens vote only and so formally express their preferences every few years. The second is that they usually cannot vote on every individual item of public business. In elections they can choose only the party whose platform of policies accommodates their priorities better than others. The direct democracy of classical Athens had neither feature.[135] Every year the Athenians could vote on the forty or more occasions when the assembly met.[136] In such a meeting, items were not bundled together as they are in today's elections: the *dēmos* heard politicians debate the options for one *probouleuma* only and voted on which option they wanted before they moved on to next item on the assembly's agenda. Without these features Athenian democracy was probably more successful than today's democracies in turning preferences into policies. There is thus no reason to doubt that the sums that the Athenian *dēmos* voted to spend on public activities were a clear reflection of their priorities.

The loss of the *arkhē* at the Peloponnesian War's end significantly reduced the income of Athens and so necessitated greater planning of its expenditure.[137] The Athenians responded by setting the annual budgets for an increasing range of public activities. By the 320s such budgets apparently covered most public spending.[138] Aristotle's pupil details how the *apodektai*, when they have received each prytany's "installments," allocate (*merizousi*) this income to the magistrates of the funds for different public activities ([Arist.] *Ath. Pol.* 48.1–2).[139] In this *merismos* ("allocation"), what each official received was laid down by a *nomos* ("law").[140] Consequently the *dēmos* could change the permanent yearly budget for a particular activity only by amending the relevant law (e.g., *IG* ii³ 327.15–23, 355.35–41, 452.41–46). "This new system shows Athens engaging in a budgeting exercise, deciding in advance how much money to make available for spending in different areas."[141]

This system appears to have been expanded slowly, as its separate funds were created one at a time. The first of them was the *stratiōtika* or military fund, whose earliest attestation is a law of 374/3 (RO 26.53–55; cf. [Dem.] 49.12, 19; 50.10).[142] Before 350 any surplus of public income at the year's end was deposited into this fund (see section entitled "Democracy," above). Among other funds, the assembly's fund for expenses is first attested in 368/7 (*IG* ii² 106.18–19), the warship-building fund in 356/5 (Dem. 22.17), and the jury-pay fund in 349/8 (39.17). Yet the *merismos* itself clearly predated these attestations, since a decree of 386 had the *apodektai* perform the same duties as they had in the 320s: they received "installments" and allocated (*merizein*) this money according to the *nomoi* or laws (RO 19.18–22).[143] Certainly this was a more advanced system for planning public spending than the previous century's ad hoc budgeting. It thus allowed fourth-century Athenians to translate their order of priorities for the *polis* more efficiently into what they spent on its different activities.

THE SYNOPSIS OF THE BOOK

This book settles public-spending debates about classical Athens as follows. Chapter 2 costs the full program of Athenian festivals. The largest of them by far were the City Dionysia and the Great Panathenaea. The first of these major festivals was celebrated each year. On it, wealthy sponsors and the *polis* itself spent 29 t. The Great Panathenaea cost 25 t., but it was celebrated every fourth year, and so its annual cost was only 6 t. The cost of a festival depended on its scale. Athenian festivals shared standard rituals. For these two major celebrations the scale of each ritual can be quantified. It is possible to compare this scale with what happened in the rest of the festival program. These comparisons suggest that the City Dionysia and the Great Panathenaea accounted for 35 percent of what the classical Athenians spent on their religious celebrations. As the combined annual cost of both festivals was 35 t., this percentage suggests that the full cost of the program of Athenian festivals was 100 t. per year. These 2.6 tons of silver per year were a lot of money. Certainly it was larger than the public income of all but the biggest Greek *poleis* ("city-states").

Chapter 3 costs the democracy. In the 420s the Athenians spent 157 t. on it each year. These 4.1 tons of silver were also a large sum. It was 50 percent more than what was spent on festivals. But the *dēmos* did not need to tap imperial tribute to raise it. In the early 420s the income of Athens was 1,000 t. per year: 600 t. of it came from the *arkhē* and 400 t. from internal sources. The *dēmos* reserved external income for wars and internal income for nonmilitary purposes. Their major areas of nonmilitary spending were festivals and politics. Elite liturgists paid for a lot of the 100 t., which was spent on the former each year. Consequently the *dēmos* could draw on more than 300 t. of public funds to pay for their democracy. Admittedly the fourth-century democracy cost less. But the 98 t. per year that was spent on it in the 370s matched festival spending. By the 330s its full cost had risen to 128 t. Without the *arkhē*, fourth-century Athenians could draw on only internal income to pay for it. If they did so, their fifth-century forebears could have done the same.

Chapter 4 costs the armed forces. The first ten years of the Peloponnesian War cost Athens considerably more than the income from its *arkhē*. Hence it had to borrow heavily. Each year these war loans ranged from 76 t. to 1,370 t. In the mid 420s the *dēmos* had to levy an annual war tax of 200 t. and increase tribute from 388 t. to 1,200 t. The Archidamian War also used up the 212 t. of the *arkhē*'s other income and the surplus of 100 t. from the state's internal income. Therefore, in the 420s the annual average of public spending on the armed forces was 1,485 t. For the rest of the Peloponnesian War it ranged between 30 and 100 percent of these

38.6 tons of silver. In the 370s the capital costs of the armed forces went from 24 t. to 7 t. per year. Their annual fixed operating costs were 133 t., while their variable operating costs went as high as 858 t. In the 370s the average of public and private spending on the armed forces was 522 t. per year. It remained roughly at this annual level of 13.6 tons of silver into the 360s.

Chapter 5 considers what these costings suggest about the priorities of the *dēmos*. In times of war, spending on the armed forces easily surpassed the combined costs of festivals and politics. In the 370s the Athenians spent 5 times more on war than on either of their other major activities. In the 420s public spending on it was 15 times as much as spending on festivals and 10 times as much as public spending on democracy. The *dēmos* had full control over this spending. Consequently the sums that they agreed to spend reflected the order of the priorities which they had for their state. This book's costings leave little doubt about what this order was. The *dēmos* judged the worship of their gods equally as important as their participation in politics. But the enormous difference between their costs and that of the armed forces suggest that the *dēmos* judged war to be of a much higher importance. This is supported by the general place of *polemos* ("war") in classical Athens. In the eyes of the Athenian *dēmos*, war always brought security, power, and other benefits. They also saw it as the opportunity to prove their manliness. This cultural militarism, the incessant warmaking of classical Athens, and the enormous costs of its wars in lives and in treasure leave no doubt that *polemos* was the overriding priority of the Athenian people.

TWO

THE COST OF FESTIVALS

With justification the classical Athenians believed that they staged more festivals than any other Greek *polis* ("city-state"). The City Dionysia and the Great Panathenaea were by far the largest of their *heortai* ("festivals") and so accounted for a significant proportion of what they spent on their program of *polis*-sponsored religious celebrations. Therefore estimating the cost of these two major festivals provides a solid base for working out their festival program. As Peter Wilson costs the City Dionysia so thoroughly, this chapter focuses on determining the cost of the Great Panathenaea. Attic farmers and wealthy sponsors paid for a lot of this *heortē*. The evidence that survives allows us to calculate what each group spent. By adding these private-spending calculations to the documented figures for public spending, this chapter establishes the cost of this second major festival. We simply lack the evidence to cost all the festivals of classical Athens, but we do know enough to estimate the scale of its two major *heortai* relative to the rest of its festival program. In classical Athens the scale of a festival largely determined its cost. This fact makes an estimate of relative scale enormously useful, as it points to the proportion of the program's full cost for which these two major celebrations accounted.

The standard ritual acts of an Athenian *heortē* were the sacrifice, the procession, the *agōnes* ("contests") for choruses and teams, and the others for individual competitors. This chapter quantifies the scale of each act at the City Dionysia and the Great Panathenaea and compares this scale to what happened in the rest of the *polis*-sponsored festivals. These comparisons allow us to estimate safely what proportion of total religious spending the two festivals consumed. Because of Wilson's costing of one major *heortē* and this chapter's costing of the other, this proportion makes possible a cost-estimate of the full program of Athenian festivals.

THE COST OF THE GREAT PANATHENAEA

The Great Panathenaea was the large-scale version of the annual festival in honor of Athena, which was held every four years. It did not mark the goddess' birthday, which is a misinterpretation going back to the nineteenth century, but commemorated the Gigantomachy and Athena's prominent role in this military victory of the Olympians over the Giants (e.g., Arist. fr. 637 Rose).[1] No other Athenian festival had a larger and more varied competitive program than this quadrennial showcase: there were *agōnes* for individuals in a wide range of athletic, equestrian, and musical events and others for choruses and tribal teams of torch racers, courageous young men, and sailors.[2] The *pompē* ("procession") of the Great Panathenaea involved thousands of citizens and foreigners and traversed the heart of the city, conveying the newly made *peplos* or robe for Athena and the so-called hecatomb for the public sacrifice. The direct costs of these ritual acts were borne by Attic farmers, the public purse, and wealthy liturgists and were on a par only with those of the City Dionysia.

The victors and placegetters in the athletic and equestrian *agōnes* of the Great Panathenaea were awarded multiple amphorae of olive oil (e.g., [Arist.] *Ath. Pol.* 60.1–3; Pind. *Nem.* 10.33–37).[3] The image of Athena, which always appeared on one side of the amphorae, evoked the festival's *aition* or mythical explanation, as it showed the goddess dancing her pyrrhic dance for the first time as part of the Olympians' celebration of their victory in the Gigantomachy (figure 2.1).[4] The winner of the men's *stadion* was probably given 80 amphorae.[5] The first prize in the chariot race for two full-grown horses was 140 amphorae (*IG* ii² 2311.67–68). The availability of prizes in such large numbers apparently attracted

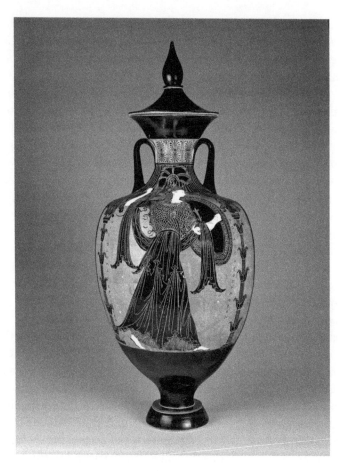

FIGURE 2.1.

Panathenaic amphora showing Athena dancing for the first time the
pyrrhic dance in celebration of the military victory of the Olympians over
the Giants, 363/2 BC, attributed to the Painter of the Wedding Procession.
Malibu, Villa Collection, J. Paul Getty Museum, Inv. No. 93.AE.55.
Photograph courtesy of the Getty Museum's Open Content Program.

numerous foreign competitors, for many of this festival's amphorae have been found in sanctuaries around the Greek world, while
several of Pindar's victory songs for non-Athenians mention their
athletic or chariot-racing victories at Athens.[6]

These amphorae had a unique shape and were especially commissioned for the Great Panathenaea, but they were only the con-
tainers of the recognized prize: the olive oil that was sacred to
Athena (e.g., [Arist.] *Ath. Pol.* 60.1; Pind. *Nem.* 10.33–37).[7] Aristotle's pupil explained how, in his day, the oil for the prizes was
raised by a general levy on the oil production of Attica's plots on
which so-called *moriai* or sacred olive trees grew, whereas, in
earlier times, it was collected directly from the sacred trees by
entrepreneurs who had bought the right to do so at a public auction ([Arist.] *Ath. Pol.* 60.2; Lys. 7.2).[8] For the Athenians these
trees were offshoots of the world's first olive tree, which Athena
had planted on the Acropolis (e.g., Eur. *Tro.* 802).[9] They were
found on "many" plots of farmed land right across Attica (Lys. 7.7,
24–25, 29).[10] In Aristotle's day the annual levy was overseen by the
eponymous archon, who handed over the oil so acquired to the
treasurers of Athena ([Arist.] *Ath. Pol.* 60.3).[11] In turn, the treasurers stored the sacred oil on the Acropolis until just before each
celebration of the quadrennial festival, when they measured it out
to the so-called *athlothetai*. This last board of magistrates is first
attested for the 440s (Plut. *Per.* 13.11) and had become the chief
administrators of the Great Panathenaea by 415/4 at the latest (*IG*
i[3] 370.66–68).[12] Aristotle's student writes ([Arist.] *Ath. Pol.* 60.1):
"They hold office for four years: they administer the procession
at the Panathenaea, and the musical contests, the athletic contests, and the horse race; they are responsible for making the robe,
and together with the council for the making of vases, and they
present the olive oil to the winning athletes."[13]

For the Great Panathenaea we have a fragmentary list of its
events and the prizes for its victors and placegetters (*IG* ii[2] 2311).[14]
This inscription is dated to the 380s on epigraphical grounds. Julia
Shear builds a strong case that its publication, the recording of
the eponymous archon's name on Panathenaic amphorae, which
manifestly begins around 380, and the means of levying oil that

Aristotle's pupil outlined were part of a general reform of the procuring of the festival's prizes, which took place sometime in the 380s.[15] Drawing on her unsurpassed collection of testimonia on this festival and her first-hand knowledge of the stone, Shear proposes a convincing restoration of this prize list, which includes the full program of the events, and most of their prizes, that are attested at Panathenaic celebrations of the early fourth century.[16] The surviving portion of this inscription mentions 819 amphorae, to which, she plausibly argues, we can add with reasonable certainty another 628 for the men's athletic contests, adding up to 1,447 prize amphorae.[17] Shear continues: "Rough extrapolation from the preserved prizes for the hippic competitions suggests that the total number of vases . . . certainly exceeded 2,000, perhaps by as much as 100 or 150 vessels."[18]

Scholars long assumed that the Panathenaic amphora held 1 *metrētēs* or 12 *choes*.[19] The *metrētēs* and *chous* were standard liquid measures of the Athenians and were equivalent to 39.40 and 3.28 liters respectively.[20] In his reappraisal of this vessel from the sixth to the fourth centuries, Martin Bentz tests this assumption by measuring the capacity of 71 surviving prizes, which, as the condition of many amphorae precludes their filling up, happens to be the most thorough study of this question to date.[21] Bentz establishes that Panathenaic prizes cluster closely around an average volume of 36.73 liters, which points strongly to the goal of filling each pot with 1 *chous* short of a *metrētēs*.[22] However, even if Athena's treasurers measured out only 11 *choes* for each amphora, the filling of 2,100 of them would have required an extraordinary 1,925 *metrētai* or 75,845 liters of olive oil.

This oil may have been raised through a general produce tax and not by purchase on the open market. Estimating as best as we can its monetary value, however, gives us a clearer idea of how much Attic farmers contributed to the Great Panathenaea. Due to the great variability in olive harvests and war-related disruptions of interstate trade, the cost of oil in classical Greece varied greatly, with recorded prices ranging from 12 dr. per *metrētēs* to several times this figure.[23] A "more common price" was probably between 16 to 18 dr., which represents the stable range of prices from the mid third century onwards.[24] If we use the figure of 17 dr. per *metrētēs*, we can thus cost this private contribution of Attic farmers to the staging of this festival at 5 t. 2,725 dr.

Additionally the Athenian *dēmos* ("people") authorized the spending of reasonably significant sums of public income on this quadrennial festival (e.g., *IG* i³ 375.3). For example, in 410/9 the treasurers of Athena handed over 5 t. 1,000 dr. to the *athlothetai* for a celebration of the Great Panathenaea and a further 5,114 dr. to the *hieropoioi* ("doers of sacred things") to pay for its regular sacrifice of 100 cows (375.5–8). According to earlier surviving accounts (370.66–68), in 415/4 Athena's treasurers gave 9 t. "to the *athlothetai* for the Panathenaea." While this sum was disbursed within days of the so-called Small Panathenaea, and so might be connected with this festival, it is far from likely that it went towards the costs of this annual version of the festival.[25] Firstly, the absence of *megala* ("great") in this entry does not rule out the quadrennial Panathenaea, as this adjective was regularly omitted in descriptions of the large-scale versions of annual festivals where it would in fact have been entirely appropriate (e.g., *IG* ii² 3022.3–4).[26] Secondly, the *athlothetai* are not otherwise attested as administering any aspect of the annual Panathenaea until the late second century (e.g., *IG* ii² 1036, 1060).[27]

What evidence we have, finally, for the public funding of the Small Panathenaea renders its consumption of such a large sum quite unlikely. In the mid-330s the Athenians created a stronger fiscal base for this annual festival by assigning to the *hieropoioi* responsible for its administration the rent from newly acquired sacred lands, which, it was optimistically hoped, would amount to 2 t. (RO 81.A.5–7, B.1–4).[28] The actual rent may have only come to 4,100 dr., but it was still sufficient to cover the festival's costliest item: the sacrificial cows for its procession (B.10–18, 23). In addition, the *dēmos* approved another 30 dr. to pay for the procession's other expenses and for the *pannukhis* or all-night celebration (B.27–37). Clearly the annual Panathenaea was a "relatively small affair."[29] As Athens in this period of expanding festival funding was contributing less than 1 t. towards this yearly version of the festival, its spending of over ten times this figure for the same purpose eighty years earlier is simply inconceivable. Consequently the most plausible explanation of these 9 t. is that they were given out to pay for the expenses that the *athlothetai* were accruing as they prepared for the Great Panathenaea of the following year. Boards of these magistrates thus appear to have received two or possibly more transfers of funds from Athena's treasurers during their four-year terms. In light of the two surviving figures we have for these transfers, this suggests that the city most probably contributed between 10 and 15 t. (and possibly more) of public funds towards each celebration of the Great Panathenaea.[30]

In view of the lacunose state of the evidence, a complete breakdown of how the *athlothetai* spent this large sum is difficult to work out. However, several of their larger expenses can be identified and estimated. For example, while Attic farmers furnished the olive oil for the Panathenaic prizes, the *athlothetai* and council of five hundred were responsible for the amphorae that were needed for its distribution as prizes ([Arist.] *Ath. Pol.* 60.1). At a public auction of 415/4, ten lots of ten second-hand Panathenaic amphorae were sold, fetching just over 3 ob. per vessel on average (*IG* i³ 422.41–60). The highest recorded price for a finely painted pot from classical Athens was 3 dr. for a hydria, which, while comparable in size to a Panathenaic amphora, usually had a lot more painted imagery.[31] Aristophanes made out that a "very good" *lekythos*, which was amongst the smallest of pots, cost 1 ob. (*Ran.* 1236). These figures suggest that a cautious cost estimate for a new Panathenaic amphora might be 1 dr. 3 ob.

The prize list of the early fourth century details other contests whose prizes were not oil but cash purses, bullion crowns, and/or cows. Thus, winners and placegetters among tribal teams and pyrrhic choruses won cows or other banqueting supplies of a set amount, costing the city 1,200 dr. in total (*IG* ii² 2311.83–93).[32] This list also records prizes of gold crowns and cash awards for winners and placegetters in the musical *agōnes*, totaling 5,200 dr. (5–22). Shear's restoration of *IG* ii² 2311 includes the tribal equestrian event of the *anthippasia* and contests for cyclic choruses, rhapsodes, and boys singing to the accompaniment of a flute or playing a *kithara*.[33] Although she does not estimate the prizes for these events, comparison with the list's known prizes and the high prestige of the rhapsodic contest suggest that these may have cost the city up to 1 t. (e.g., Pl. *Ion* 535e4–536). As the average of the recorded prices for a cow in classical Athens was 72 dr., another 1 t. 1,200 dr. of public funds was needed to pay for the festival's hundred-cow sacrifice.[34]

Finally, the *athlothetai* had to pay for the preparations for, and equipment of, the festival's *pompē*. For such expenses the city of the later fourth century gave 1 t. 4,000 dr. to the *epimelētai* ("supervisors") in charge of the procession of the City Dionysia ([Arist.] *Ath. Pol.* 56.4; cf. Dem. 21.15). The *pompē* of the Great Panathenaea was always as grand and involved two expenses that the supervisors of the City Dionysia never faced: the setting up of *ikria* ("wooden stands") for spectators in the *agora* ("marketplace") and the making of the *peplos* ([Arist.] *Ath. Pol.* 60.1), which was, by all accounts, "an elaborate gift for Athena."[35] Thus, this procession of the Great Panathenaea may have cost the city in excess of 2 t.

Some of the direct costs of the festival were borne directly by wealthy citizens who volunteered or were, if necessary, conscripted to pay for the training and the equipping of its choruses and tribal teams.[36] Most of the figures that we have for such festival liturgies come from a legal speech of 404/3. The speaker of Lysias 21 opened his defense against a charge of financial misconduct as a magistrate by costing his own liturgies.[37] Certainly his "liturgical career is unique in its intensity": from 411/0 to 404/3 he paid for 17 liturgies at a combined cost of nearly 10 t.[38] Importantly, however, while no other individual is known to have performed as many public services in such a short period, the amounts that he spent on individual liturgies do not appear to have been out of the ordinary.[39] For example, in each of the years when he served as a trierarch, he spent 5,163 dr., which is very close to the average of the surviving figures for this military liturgy and is by no means the highest of them.[40] Likewise, the 3,000 dr. that this speaker paid for a tragic chorus in 411/0 parallels the 5,000 dr. that another liturgist spent performing the same liturgy twice in the late 390s (Lys. 19.42, 21.1).

In view of the crises that the city weathered during these years, the comparability of these costs—along with the stable liturgical spending that Lysias 21 itself records—is quite remarkable.[41] They bear out the "overriding importance" that the Athenians placed in honoring their deities and suggest an underlying stability in festival-related spending during this tumultuous period of Athenian history.[42] As they appear to be unexceptional, the amounts of private money that the speaker of Lysias 21 spent as a liturgist can be safely used for estimating private spending on the Great Panathenaea's choruses and teams.

The full program of these contests for groups is securely attested for the 380s, for although some of the section of *IG* ii² 2311 that details these events has not survived, enough external evidence exists for restoring these missing lines. In classical Athens the most popular of the tribally organized contests was clearly the torch race (e.g., Aesch. *Ag.* 312–314; Ar. *Ran.* 1087–1098).[43] By the early fourth century this event had long been part of both versions of the Panathenaea and the yearly festivals for Hephaestus and Prometheus (e.g., *IG* i³ 82.31–35, ii² 2311.88–89).[44] The painters of the city's pots depicted no other athletic event in as much detail as they did the torch race.[45] As was the case with two other of his festival liturgies, the speaker of Lysias 21 served as a *gumnasiarkhos* ("athletics-training sponsor") but for only a team of torch racers that competed at another festival. Victorious liturgists at the Great Panathenaea certainly won much greater prestige, which they assiduously publicized (e.g., [Andoc.] 4.42; *IG* ii² 3019, 3022), than those who succeeded in the same events at other religious celebrations. This means that the athletic-training sponsors and *khorēgoi* ("chorus sponsors") at Athena's festival were probably willing to spend more than they would for other gods.[46] Consequently the 1,200 dr. that the speaker of Lysias 21 devoted to the torch race of the Prometheia serves as a safe minimum figure for this liturgy at the Great Panathenaea.

For the victorious tribe in the *hamilla neōn* ("race of ships") the prize list of the 380s records as prizes 300 dr. for three cows and another 200 dr. for a feast (*IG* ii² 2311.90–92).[47] The total value of these prizes is five times more than that for other group events (84–89), which suggests that there were considerably more competitors in the ship race than in the choral and other team events. This amount—along with *naus* strictly denoting a ship of war (e.g., Xen. *Hell.* 5.4.34–35)—points to the use of triremes for this event in the Panathenaic games.[48] If this is correct, Lysias 21 provides a minimum cost for readying such a crew for competition: the speaker spent 1,500 dr. competing (*hamillōmenos*) with a trireme at Sunium (5). That this ship race took place at Sunium rules out any possible association with the Great Panathenaea.[49]

Another well-attested event of the Panathenaic games of this period is the *anthippasia*, which saw the tribal corps of the city's cavalrymen charge each other in a mock battle.[50] Liturgical funding was probably not required for this equestrian event, because training for, and participation in, the *anthippasia* were a regular part of cavalry service (Xen. *Eq. Mag.* 3.1, 10–14), while its victory monuments were set up by the winning tribe or the commander of its cavalry unit (e.g., *IG* ii² 3130).[51]

The *purrhikhē* was an event for choristers wearing a hoplite helmet and bearing a spear and shield (figure 2.2).[52] The classical Athenians believed that Athena had invented it as part of the victory celebration of the Olympians after the Gigantomachy (e.g., Aesch. *Eum.* 292–296).[53] At the Great Panathenaea of the 380s there were separate contests in the pyrrhic chorus for three age classes (*IG* ii² 2311.84–86). Its *khorēgiai* or chorus sponsorships cost 800 dr. (Lys. 21.1). The festival probably also sported dithyrambic contests, as was the case at its smaller celebration (Lys. 21.2; [Xen.] *Ath. Pol.* 3.4).[54] Certainly there would have been enough space in the prize list's lost portion to detail prizes for this second set of choruses.[55] Two age classes rather than the three of the *purrhikhē* are more likely for this event, since separate contests for "boys" and "men" are securely attested for the dithyramb at the City Dionysia and Thargelia (e.g., [Arist.] *Ath. Pol.* 56.3; *IG* ii² 1138). A minimum cost for this liturgy is the 300 dr., which the speaker of Lysias 21 spent on the same event at the Small Panathenaea of 409/8 (2).

Shear defends the longstanding assumption that each of the ten Cleisthenic tribes entered choruses in the pyrrhic contests.[56] She argues for such a tribal organization on the grounds that this

FIGURE 2.2.
Base of the victory monument of Artabos showing him as a victorious chorus sponsor standing beside his chorus of pyrrhic dancers, 323/2 BC. Athens, Acropolis Museum, Inv. No. 1338. Photograph courtesy of H. R. Goette.

event appears on the list of prizes under the same heading as the *euandria* ("manliness contest") and the torch race (*IG* ii² 2311.83) and in lines 87 to 89 the prizes for these last two events are described as being "for the winning tribe."[57] For her the absence of a comparable description in the lines concerning the armed dance (84–86) was due only to a lack of space on the stone. As none of the other testimonia for the *purrhikhē*'s organization mentions tribes (Isae. 5.36; Lys. 21.2, 4; *IG* ii² 3025, 3026; *SEG* xxiii.103), others question strongly any such tribal arrangement.[58] Paola Ceccarelli puts the case against it beyond doubt: "While it may be possible to find an *ad hoc* explanation for the failure of every one of these documents to mention a tribe in connection with pyrrhic competitions, the only comprehensive explanation is to assume that they were not organized on a tribal basis."[59] The same objection can be made against the assumption that the dithyrambs of the Small and Great Panathenaea were also organized by tribes.[60] The ancient testimonia do not mention tribes (Lys. 21.2; [Xen.] *Ath. Pol.* 3.4).

Thus, we are forced to estimate the number of the liturgies that were required for the *purrhikhē* and cyclic choruses, because we have no reason to believe that they were organized by tribes and otherwise lack any direct evidence for their number. Tellingly the Athenian people took note of how pyrrhic *khorēgoi* performed: jurors apparently had significantly less *kharis* ("gratitude") for a sponsor when they knew that his choristers had come dead last (Isae. 5.36), whereas a winner could be publicly honored and praised for performing his liturgy "well and with zeal" (e.g., *SEG* xxxiv.103.2–8).[61] Sponsors of the *purrhikhē* also thought winning worth publicizing by commissioning their own victory monuments (figure 2.2).[62] All of this suggests that victory was far from assured: individual sponsors and their pyrrhic choristers faced real competition when they competed in their age class. Consequently it is likely that the number of choruses and hence *khorēgoi* in a pyrrhic contest never fell below three.[63] This also seems a safe minimum for the dithyrambic event ([Plut.] *Dec. Orat.* 842a).[64]

A different type of estimate is needed for calculating private spending on the *euandria* ([Arist.] *Ath. Pol.* 60.3; Ath. 13.565f; *IG* ii² 2311.87). This final team event of the Great Panathenaea of the 380s may certainly have been organized by tribes and hence required ten wealthy sponsors, but we do not have recorded figures for this festival liturgy nor, for that matter, enough evidence to reconstruct what this *agōn* actually entailed.[65] Fortunately a pointer to the relative cost of training this tribal team exists: those of its liturgists who had won happily publicized their victories, putting them on a par with their successes as *gumnasiarkhoi* ([Andoc.] 4.42; *IG* ii² 3022).[66] This implies that the costs of these tribal liturgies were at least of a similar scale. Since the lowest figure that we have for a festival liturgy is 300 dr. (Lys. 21.2) and the only one for a torch race is 1,200 dr. (3–4), a cautious estimate for preparing a team for the *euandria* might be 800 dr., which is also the cost of a pyrrhic chorus at the Great Panathenaea (1). On the basis of the

TABLE 2.1. THE COST OF THE GREAT PANATHENAEA IN THE 380S

Public Expenditure	12 t. 3,000 dr.
Market Value of the Olive Oil for the Prizes	5 t. 2,725 dr.
Festival Liturgies	7 t. 2,000 dr.

10 *gumnasiarkhiai* for the torch race at 1,200 dr.
each = 2 t.
10 liturgies for the ship race at 1,500 dr. each = 2 t.
3,000 dr.
9 *khorēgiai* for the pyrrhic choruses at 800 dr. each =
1 t. 1,200 dr.
6 *khorēgiai* for the cyclic choruses at 300 dr. each =
1,800 dr.
10 liturgies for the *euandria* at 800 dr. each =
1 t. 2,000 dr.

TOTAL	25 t. 1,725 dr.
ANNUAL COST	6 t. 1,931 dr.

numbers and the costings of liturgies that we have worked out, the total of this private spending by wealthy liturgists comes to 7 t. 2,000 dr.

Table 2.1 summarizes my costing of the Great Panathenaea in the 380s. Importantly it parallels the cost estimate of the City Dionysia by Wilson.[67] I estimate that each celebration of Athena's festival cost 25 t. 1,725 dr. Wilson costs the other showcase of classical Athens at 28 t. 5,200 dr. Attic farmers and wealthy liturgists covered about half of the Great Panathenaea's cost. Likewise, Wilson shows that private spending on the City Dionysia roughly matched what the *polis* spent. Consequently our independent costings of the two major *heortai* of classical Athens corroborate each other. Averaged over a four-year period, the cost of the public and private spending on the Great Panathenaea was 6 t. 1,931 dr. per year.

THE RELATIVE SCALE OF THE REST
OF THE FESTIVAL PROGRAM

The classical Athenians staged *polis*-sponsored festivals and public sacrifices regularly throughout the year and believed with some justification that they had more of them than any other Greek city.[68] *Heortai* of course gave their human participants *terpsis* or delight and respite from, among other toils, the *ponoi* of war (e.g., Pl. *Leg.* 653d; Thuc. 2.38.1).[69] The opportunities that they gave for watching sport, feasting on meat, and carousing more generally encouraged happiness (Diod. Sic. 12.26.4). They also helped to maintain, it was believed, the *kharis* of their objects of worship.[70] The scale of the Athenian program of *polis*-level festivals is evident in the so-called *dermatikon* accounts.[71] They record the income that Athens gained from the sale of the hides of cows that it had sacrificed between 334/3 and 331/0.[72]

For each year, the *dermatikon* accounts cover sixteen festivals and sacrifices, listing the proceeds from the sales of hides after each celebration (*IG* ii² 1496.68–151). We have already noted how the average cost of a cow was 72 dr. (see "The Cost of the Great Panathenaea," above). The average price of a cowhide in classical Athens was probably 7 dr.[73] In light of these costs known for a cow and cowhide, these accounts provide a solid platform for calculating how much Athens of the 330s spent on public sacrifices and the percentage of this cost the City Dionysia and Great Panathenaea accounted for.[74] Unfortunately the sale figures for the Panathenaea, the annual festival of the Eleusinia, and the sacrifice to Hermes Hegemonius are lost or incomplete.[75] We have already seen that a contemporary inscription authorizes the spending of 4,100 dr. on the major sacrifice for the Small Panathenaea (RO 81.B.16–17, 23–24). This would have paid for 57 cows, and the 100-cow sacrifice of the Great Panathenaea is securely attested.[76] As

TABLE 2.2. ANNUAL FIGURES FOR PUBLIC
SACRIFICES IN THE 330S

Celebration	Hide Sales	Cows	Cost
Sacrifice to *Eirēnē*	794 dr.	113	1 t. 2,136 dr.
Panathenaea	—	43	3,096 dr.
Great Panathenaea	—	25	1,800 dr.
Eleusinia	—	84	1 t. 48 dr.
Sacrifice to *Dēmokratia*	414 dr.	59	4,248 dr.
Epidauria	1,000 dr.	143	1 t. 4,296 dr.
Theseia	1,183 dr.	169	2 t. 168 dr.
Dionysia of the Piraeus	311 dr.	44	3,168 dr.
Lenaea	106 dr.	15	1,080 dr.
Sacrifice to *Agathē Tukhē*	131 dr.	19	1,368 dr.
Asclepieia	284 dr.	41	2,952 dr.
City Dionysia	557 dr.	80	5,760 dr.
Olympieia	601 dr.	86	1 t. 192 dr.
Sacrifice to Hermes Hegemonius	—	84	1 t. 48 dr.
Bendideia	457 dr.	65	4,680 dr.
Sacrifice to Zeus the Saviour	1831 dr.	262	3 t. 864 dr.
TOTALS		1,332	15 t. 5,902 dr.

the latter festival was the large-scale version that was celebrated every four years, these sacrifices should be averaged over the quadrennium to allow for a comparison with the other annual celebrations of the *dermatikon* accounts. In the absence of evidence for the size of public sacrifices at Eleusis and for Hermes Hegemonius, we can use for them only the average size of attested public sacrifices. Table 2.2 details the results of my calculations: Athens of the 330s spent 15 t. 5,902 dr. publicly sacrificing some 1,332 cows each year. The sacrifices of the City Dionysia and the Great Panathenaea represented only 8 percent of these two figures.[77]

Certainly the *dermatikon* accounts shed much light on the extent of the religious life of the Athenian *polis* and on its remarkable supplementation of the local food supply. But they do not actually tell us what percentage of the festival program's *full* cost was spent on these two major festivals. Manifestly, relative spending on them was considerably higher than 8 percent. Two of the public sacrifices that these accounts mention were probably recent additions to the festival program, while its first celebration for Dionysus, namely, the Dionysia of the Piraeus, cannot be part of our calculations (*IG* ii² 1496.70–73).[78] This festival—like other celebrations of the Rural Dionysia (e.g., *IG* i³ 254; ii² 1206)—was administered and funded primarily by demes and hence was not a *polis*-level celebration.[79] Of course the standard ritual acts of an Athenian festival were the *thusia* ("sacrifice"), *pompē*, *agōnes* for choruses and tribal teams, and other competitions for individuals.[80] In classical Athens most *heortai* had *agōnes* in athletics, horsemanship, drama, music, or, more often than not, in a combination of these activities.[81] Indeed Robin Osborne concludes that "competition was a basic element of the worship of the gods at Athens, and that the more grand the worship offered the more likely it was to include something competitive."[82] In spite of this, several Athenian religious celebrations lacked *agōnes*, and a handful did not even have a *pompē*. Indeed in four of the *dermatikon* accounts' festivals, a god is honored by a *thusia* alone, which would have been cheaper than a full-blown *heortē*.[83] Moreover, the other ritual acts regularly cost more than the sacrifice, while the amounts they used up at the City Dionysia and Great Panathenaea were disproportionate to the rest of the festival program.[84]

Certainly the *pompai* ("processions") of these two festivals were the most elaborate and the most costly of the twelve or so that the city staged.[85] Among their thousands of participants were groups representing citizens of different ages, metics, and women, each of whom carried distinct ritual equipment, military and civilian magistrates, delegates of the demes, and private individuals.[86] In the Great Panathenaea, hoplites and the entire cavalry corps processed as well (figures 2.3 and 2.4).[87] During the fifth century it was only to these processions that Athens ordered its allies and colonists to send delegates, bearing a cow and hoplite panoply for Athena and large phalluses for Dionysus (e.g.,

IG i³ 14.2–8, 34.41–43, 46.15–17, 71.55–58).⁸⁸ The city spent several talents equipping and staging these ritual acts (see "The Cost of the Great Panathenaea," above). That they were several times larger than the other *pompai* is shown by their unique administration: the procession of the City Dionysia was administered by the eponymous archon and a dedicated board of supervisors ([Arist.] *Ath. Pol.* 56.3–4; Dem. 23.15) and that of the Great Panathenaea by city-based *athlothetai* (e.g., [Arist.] *Ath. Pol.* 60.1–3; *IG* i³ 378.14–15).⁸⁹ This latter board of ten magistrates began its preparations four years in advance of the Panathenaic games and also managed the contests, the making of prizes and Athena's robe, and the awarding of winners ([Arist.] *Ath. Pol.* 49.3, 60.1). No other religious celebration had its own board of *polis*-based magistrates.

The Athenian *dēmos* compelled their wealthy citizens to pay for a large part of the running costs of their festival program (e.g., Xen. *Oec.* 2.6).⁹⁰ The *lampadēphoroi* ("torch racers") of the Great Panathenaea, Hephaesteia, and Prometheia competed and trained as part of teams that had been drawn from the Cleisthenic tribes. The cost of training each of these ten teams fell to a wealthy citizen serving as a *gumnasiarkhos* (e.g., Xen. *Vect.* 4.51–52). A *khorēgos* did the same for each of the choruses that competed in the city's dramatic and dithyrambic contests (e.g., [Arist.] *Ath. Pol.* 56.2–3). In addition, wealthy citizens were responsible for a handful of other liturgies to do with the city's *heortai* (e.g., Dem. 21.156; Lys. 21.5). The number of these public services obviously increased as the *dēmos* authorized the expansion of its *polis*-level festivals.

Elite Athenians were placed under considerable social pressure to undertake such liturgies. As far as the Athenian *dēmos* were concerned, it was the duty of wealthy citizens to do so (e.g., Ar. *Lys.* 653–654; Dem. 42.22; Lys. 27.10). Thus elite citizens who sought to be politicians found that they could consolidate their popularity by performing liturgies on a lavish scale.⁹¹ Others who were involved in legal *agōnes* or disputes sought to build up the *kharis* towards themselves on the part of lower-class jurors by cataloguing the liturgies and other *agatha* ("benefactions") that they had performed for the city (e.g., Lys. 12.38, 30.1).⁹² Failure to meet this perceived duty or even the carrying out of these pub-

43

FIGURE 2.3.

Relief block of the Parthenon frieze showing members of the cavalry corps riding in the procession of the Great Panathenaea, which is depicted on Athena's temple on the Acropolis, 447/6–432/1 BC. Athens, Acropolis Museum, Inv. No. 862, Block No. North XXXVI Jenkins. Photograph courtesy of H. R. Goette.

lic services half-heartedly left wealthy citizens open to vilification by those who opposed them in a legal or political *agōn* (e.g., Din. 1.25–26; Isae. 5.36; cf. Dem. 27.46). These practices of the democracy may have ensured that many wealthy Athenians volunteered or were informally encouraged by *polis* or tribal officials to be festival liturgists or trierarchs. Nonetheless, legal means also existed to compel individuals to perform them if further numbers were required.[93]

This private spending was also hugely disproportionate at the City Dionysia and the Great Panathenaea. In a legal court speech of 355/4, Demosthenes claimed that there were 60 festival liturgies in any one year (20.21). Böckh judged this claim "hardly cred-

FIGURE 2.4.
Relief block of the Parthenon frieze, continuing on the adjoining block showing the line of cavalrymen, 447/6–432/1 BC. London, British Museum, Block No. North XXXVII Jenkins. Photograph courtesy of H. R. Goette.

ible" but never investigated the actual numbers of liturgies at each festival to prove his claim properly.[94] The first to do so was John Davies about fifty years ago.[95] Table 2.3 details his findings, which clearly vindicate Böckh's judgment: during the 350s, festival liturgies added up to 97 annually, rising to 118 in the years of the Great Panathenaea.[96] Crucially they also suggest that the City Dionysia had 29 percent of these liturgies in three out of four years, while the two festivals together accounted for 59 percent of the total number of liturgies.[97]

The Great Panathenaea also supported an enormous number of individual competitions. The prize list of the early fourth century details 27 events for such contenders (*IG* ii² 2311).[98] This fes-

TABLE 2.3.
ANNUAL NUMBER OF FESTIVAL
LITURGIES IN THE 350S

Festival	Liturgies	
City Dionysia	28	
Lenaea	7	
Thargelia	10	
Hephaesteia	10	
Prometheia	10	
(Great) Panathenaea	19	(40)
Arrhephoria	1	
Amphiareia	10	
Festivals outside Athens	2	
TOTAL	97 (118)	

tival followed the normal practice of running separate contests for different age classes, but its awarding of prizes to placegetters as well as victors set it apart from other games.[99] For individuals the festival of the 380s thus had 39 contests and 81 prizes, whose combined monetary value was probably 7 t. 2,374 dr. (see "The Cost of the Great Panathenaea," above). This program of *agōnes* for individuals was more extensive than even the Olympic Games, which helps to explain why Athena's festival took up ten days, lasting far longer than any other Athenian festival.[100] The paucity of evidence for Attica's three other games complicates our calculation of the relative weight of Panathenaic spending on contests for individuals.[101] These three other sporting festivals were the Eleusinia, the Heracleia at Marathon, and the Brauronia. Yet what we can safely say of their scale strongly suggests that the Great Panathenaea used up the lion's share of public expenditure on this class of ritual acts.

The games of the Eleusinia go back to the early years of Athenian democracy (e.g., Pind. *Isthm.* 1.57, *Ol.* 9.99, 13.110; *IG* i³ 988).[102] But the earliest evidence for their frequency and the scope of their events is the later fourth-century accounts of the three supervisors of Eleusis and the treasurers of Demeter and Persephone (*IG* ii² 1672).[103] After elaborating the sanctuary's income and expenditure, they record the amount of wheat that had been received as rent on its sacred lands and how it was spent between 332/1 and 329/8 (252–261). Seventy *medimnoi* of wheat were given out as prizes for two celebrations of a *trietēris* or two-year version of the festival (258–259) and probably another 70 *medimnoi* for a four-year version (258–260; cf. 261).[104] Both versions, according to the accounts, had horse races and contests in athletics, music, and "ancestral" events (258–260). As they next mention a horse race recently "added by an assembly-decree" (261), these biennial and quadrennial celebrations undoubtedly predate the expansion of preexisting contests that Lycurgus and others championed from the mid-330s.[105]

By the early fourth century, Athens had been staging for nearly a century annual "contests in athletics, equestrian events and music of every sort" as part of its heroization of its war dead (Pl. *Menex.* 249b; cf. Diod. Sic. 11.33.3).[106] As prizes, the victors of these games took home bronze hydrias and *lebetes* (*IG* i³ 523–525).[107] Finally, the quadrennial festival of Heracles at Marathon had athletic and musical *agōnes*, whose participants competed "over silver cups" (Pind. *Ol.* 9.90; cf. *Nem.* 9.51–53).[108]

Frustratingly there is no direct evidence for the number of contests at any of these *heortai*. Nevertheless, we have two pointers to the relative size of their programs. First, the city had far less administrative capacity to plan for, and to stage, these festivals than it did for the Great Panathenaea. The Eleusinia and Marathon's Heracleia were administered by the so-called annual *hieropoioi*, who also had responsibility for several other festivals and public sacrifices.[109] Likewise the annually appointed polemarch had much more to do than just organize the *agōnes* for the war dead ([Arist.] *Ath. Pol.* 58.1–3). As a consequence, the city most probably could not have staged contests at these festivals that were more than half the scale of those of the Great Panathenaea. However, a second fact points to these games running close to or at this maximum of twenty contests: they were clearly extensive enough to attract foreign competitors. The songs of Pindar mentioning the games of Eleusis and Marathon celebrated the victories of non-Athenians (see above), while one of the three surviving bronze prizes from the games for the war dead was found in a cemetery outside Thessaloniki.[110]

Nonetheless, the prizes of these three competitive *heortai* were of significantly less value than those of Athena's festival. The prizes of wheat at the biennial and quadrennial versions of the Eleusinia had a monetary value of 210 dr. and 420 dr. respectively.[111] The silver *phialai* or drinking cups for the Heracleia would have cost no more than 4,000 dr., and the bronze vessels of the funeral games, 1,000 dr.[112] When these maximum amounts and the figures for the Great Panathenaea are averaged out on an annual basis, Athena's festival ends taking up 19 percent of all of the contests for individuals and a staggering 83 percent of the monetary value of their prizes.[113]

THE FULL COST OF FESTIVALS

In his unflattering comparison of his state's staging of festivals and its warmaking, Demosthenes understandably focused on the City Dionysia and the Great Panathenaea (4.35–37). Considerably more time and effort went into staging these two showcases.[114] They also used up a larger amount of public and private money: Wilson's costing of the City Dionysia and mine of the Great Panathenaea suggest 35 t. 1,131 dr. per year. The calculations in this chapter of the relative scale of these two *heortai* now allow us to estimate the percentage of the festival program's full cost that they accounted for. Their sacrifices were — we have seen — more than 8 percent of the cows that the Athenian *polis* sacrificed at its festivals every year. Their *pompai* were several times larger than each of the twelve or so other processions that the *polis* staged. The City Dionysia accounted for 29 percent of festival liturgies in three out of four years, while together the two *heortai* accounted for 59 percent. The contests, finally, for individuals at the Great Panathenaea represented 19 percent of all such *agōnes* and 83 percent of the monetary value of their prizes.

On the basis of these relative figures, a cautious estimate of the proportion of the full cost of festivals that the City Dionysia and the Great Panathenaea consumed would appear to be 35 percent. In turn, this percentage suggests that the entire program of *polis*-sponsored festivals cost 100 t. 3,231 dr. This was indeed a large sum. We will see how it was comparable to what fourth-century Athenians spent on running their democracy.[115] Certainly it was far larger than the budget of all but the very biggest of Greek *poleis*.[116]

Athens was the leading cultural center of the classical Greek world. The disciplines of drama, oratory, literature, and the visual arts were developed to a far higher level of quality in this city-state than any other. Ever since Johann Winckelmann—the eighteenth-century pioneer of Classical Archaeology—this Athenian cultural revolution has been interpreted as a direct result of the democracy.[117] Certainly the requirement of *khorēgoi* and poets to win over mass audiences drove rapid innovations in comedy, tragedy, satyric drama, and dithyramb.[118] Athenian plays in particular were performed as part of *agōnes* at the City Dionysia and the Lenaea.[119] Although the adjudicating of which poet had won his *agōn* was formally in the hands of ten judges, they clearly took their cue from how the thousands of theatergoers had responded to each play (e.g., [Andoc.] 4.20–21; Ar. *Av.* 444–447, *Ran.* 771–780).[120] By regularly attending such *agōnes*, the Athenians continually enhanced their appreciation of drama.[121] Consequently *khorēgoi* and poets found a competitive advantage by pushing the boundaries of their genre. Yet this chapter's high estimate of the full cost of Athenian festivals reveals two more reasons for the cultural innovations of classical Athens. They were the extraordinary wealth of this *polis* and its upper class and the decision that its people regularly made that both should spend heavily on festival-based contests.

Of course Athens also spent public funds on its religious sanctuaries. They housed cult statues, festival equipment, and the sacred monies that paid for them. It is simply not possible to estimate this capital cost of state religion as we have its fixed operating costs. But what is known about the temples of classical Athens suggests that from 430 to 350 its *dēmos* spent vastly less on them than on its program of festivals. Unsurprisingly, fifth-century Athenians most generously funded the temple for Athena on the Acropolis that Pericles had proposed (e.g., Plut. *Per.* 12.1–13.6). The building of the Parthenon went from 447/6 to 432/1 (*IG* i³ 436–451, 453–460).[122] Yet by 438/7 enough of it had been completed for the goddess' gold-and-ivory statue to be installed (Paus. 1.24.5–7). At this point most of the Parthenon's builders were transferred to the Propylaea, where they worked for five more years (Plut. *Per.* 13.7; *IG* i³ 462–466).[123] The best possible cost estimates of these two religious buildings are 460 t. and 300 t. respectively.[124] Over the 15 years that it took to complete the largest of them their sum averages out at 51 t. per annum. This period also saw building in ten other Athenian sanctuaries.[125] The uncertainties about these temples make the estimating of their costs immensely difficult. Yet on the basis of what survives, it is hard to see how they could have been more expensive than the works on the Acropolis.

The astronomical cost of the Peloponnesian War abruptly ended most public building.[126] Those on which work continued after 432/1 were also on a significantly smaller scale.[127] During this thirty-year war only six religious buildings were completed in Attica.[128] The temple of Athena Nike is a good example: it was a fiftieth of the Parthenon's size.[129] Public building continued on this small scale until the fourth century's third quarter.[130] By then public finances had recovered from the costly Social War.[131] This made it significantly easier for Eubulus and Lycurgus to convince the *dēmos* to invest heavily again in their sanctuaries (e.g., Plut. *Mor.* 852c).[132] Consequently temple building peaked on either side of the eighty years on which this book focuses.[133] From 430 to 350 the Athenians probably spent less by an order of magnitude on this capital cost than they did on their program of *polis*-sponsored festivals. Böckh held that the temples of classical Athens "were constructed at so great an expense, that they could not have been attempted without the treasure derived from the tributes."[134] He claimed too that "their maintenance alone required a consider-able standing expense." The publication of the Parthenon build-ing accounts by W. B. Dinsmoor in 1913 refuted his first claim, as they showed that the *hellēnotamiai* ("treasurers of Greece"), who managed the empire's treasury, contributed only small sums to this project.[135] The discovery of the *Constitution of the Athenians* by Aristotle's pupil disproved his second claim, for it recorded that in the 320s Athens budgeted only 3,000 dr. per year for the repairing of its temples ([Arist.] *Ath. Pol.* 50.1).

THREE

THE COST OF DEMOCRACY

Ancient historians fiercely debate how the classical Athenians paid for their system of government. Certainly the *dēmos* ("people") spent a lot of public funds on it. This was largely the result of their decision to pay themselves to run the democracy. In the 450s they voted to introduce *misthos* ("pay") for jurors. In the 440s or the 430s they began to pay councilors and magistrates. By the 390s the *dēmos* were drawing pay to attend assembly meetings. They also found other ways to subsidize their political participation. Athenian *arkhontes* ("magistrates") were required to keep accounts. Many poor Athenians were not capable of fulfilling this duty because of their restricted schooling. Consequently they were disinclined to serve as magistrates. The *dēmos* removed this barrier to participation by giving boards of magistrates *hupogrammateis* or undersecretaries. In addition, they gave *arkhontes* public slaves to assist them to fulfill their other duties and a costly incentives scheme. Because of this range of subsidization, Pericles claimed with some justification that poverty in classical Athens was no barrier to political participation (Thuc. 2.37.1). Some ancient historians persist with the view that Böckh had on how the Athenians paid for these fixed operating costs. They argue that the *dēmos* met them only by drawing on the income from their *arkhē* ("empire"). But others argue just as strongly that Athenian democracy never relied on this external income.

This chapter aims to settle this public-spending debate by estimating the running cost of Athenian democracy in the fifth century. We do not have reliable documented figures for this category of public spending as we do for the Great Panathenaea. Therefore, each of the democracy's institutions can be costed only on the basis of its general parameters. These were the number of days when it operated each year, the number of Athenians who participated in it when it did, and the daily amount they drew as *misthos*. Working out the cost of the fourth-century democracy also helps us to adjudicate this debate. Without the *arkhē*, postwar Athenians could pay for it only with their internal income. If the cost of the democracy was the same in both centuries, this is significant, for it suggests that their fifth-century forebears could have done the same, namely, relied solely on internal sources. This book costs the armed forces of Athens in the 420s and the 370s and gives a cost estimate of its festivals that is valid for both decades. By costing its democracy in the same two decades it thus enables both a settling of this debate and a comparison of what the Athenians spent on their three major public activities. Nevertheless, working back from the better-documented 330s will assist in calculating fixed operating costs of Athenian democracy in the 420s and the 370s. Consequently this chapter also costs Athenian democracy in the 330s.

JURORS

The first form of remuneration that the classical Athenians introduced to compensate themselves for participating in their democracy was *misthos* for jury service, which Pericles pushed through in the 450s.[1] *Misthos* of 3 ob. per day was first mentioned by Aristophanes in his *Knights* of 425/4 (51, 255–256, 800; cf. 797–798). Four scholia on other comedies of his suggest that it was Cleon who was responsible for raising jury pay from 2 to 3 ob.[2] The third of these notes adds that he did so "as a general when the war against the Lacedaemonians was going well," which points to a date for this pay increase immediately after his military success at Sphacteria in the summer of 425 (Thuc. 4.24–41).[3] Jury pay was abolished during the regime of the Four Hundred and probably again in the second short period of oligarchy at the end of the Peloponnesian War ([Arist.] *Ath. Pol.* 29.5).[4] With the restoration of the democracy in 404/3 it was quickly reintroduced at the former rate of 3 ob. per day (e.g., Ar. *Eccl.* 683–688, *Plut.* 277), where it remained until the democracy's overthrow by the Macedonians in 322/1 ([Arist.] *Ath. Pol.* 62.2). Thus, the same daily rate can be used for costing jury pay in the 420s, the 370s, and the 330s.

In his *Wasps* of 423/2 Aristophanes estimated the cost of jury pay at 150 t. per year (660–663). In doing so, he assumed that the lawcourts sat for 300 days each year and always required the service of every last one of the 6,000 citizens who had been selected by lot for jury service for the year.[5] Both assumptions, clearly, were comic exaggerations.[6] The lawcourts did not sit for so many days. The Attic year had about 195 working days, of which 40 or so were used for assembly meetings, about 60 days for the city's program of annual festivals, and about 80 days for monthly public sacrifices.[7] In addition the days on which the council of the Areopagus heard lawsuits for murder were considered *hēmerai apophrades* ("taboo days"), which possibly numbered about 15.[8] The lawcourts did not sit on *hēmerai apophrades* nor on days when the assembly met (Dem. 24.80) or a yearly *heortē* ("festival") was celebrated (e.g., Ar. *Thesm.* 78–80; Lys. 26.6; [Xen.] *Ath. Pol.* 3.8), but they regularly did sit on days when monthly public sacrifices were offered (e.g., Dem. 42.5; *IG* ii² 1629.204–212, 1678.27–28).[9] Because the lawcourts presumably opened only during monthly festivals, since the working days were proving to be insufficient for getting through lawsuits, the theoretical maximum number of days they could use was 235 per year.[10] Yet it is clear that they met less often than this maximum, because magistrates in charge of the lawcourts set the days on which they would be open (e.g., Ar. *Vesp.* 304–306; [Arist.] *Ath. Pol.* 54.1). This would have been unnecessary if they sat during every monthly public sacrifice.[11] Hansen plausibly suggests that the lawcourts would have been in session on 200 days of the year.[12]

On the days when they did sit, the lawcourts did not employ 6,000 jurors. The yearly selection of them by lot was supplemented by the selection of the number of jurors who were required each day.[13] In the fifth century the 6,000 who had been chosen for jury service were divided into groups, and each group was allocated to the lawcourt of the same magistrate for the whole year (e.g., Antiph. 6.21–23; Ar. *Vesp.* 240–241). Those who wished to serve on a particular day queued in front of their lawcourt, before it opened, and were allowed to enter until the required number was met, at which point a sign would be raised to indicate that the lawcourt was full (e.g., Ar. *Vesp.* 240–241, 688–690, 774–775). From the early 370s, by contrast, on days when lawsuits were being heard, lotteries were used both to determine which of those jurors who wished to serve on the day would do so and to assign those who had been so selected to the lawcourts that were in session (e.g., Ar. *Eccl.* 681–690, *Plut.* 277, 972). Jurors received their *misthos* only when they had decided the last of the day's lawsuits (Ar. *Vesp.* 694; [Arist.] *Ath. Pol.* 69.2).[14]

In the 330s how many Athenians normally sat each day in the lawcourts? The *Constitution of the Athenians* indicates that *dikai* ("private lawsuits") had a jury of 201, if the amount in dispute was less than 1,000 dr., and 401, if it was more (53.3), while *graphai* ("indictments for public offenses") were normally judged by 501 jurors (68.1). But there were examples of *graphai* whose juries were several times larger (e.g., Andoc. 1.17; Dem. 24.9).[15] Thus an average-sized jury was probably 401. In the same period, a lottery was conducted for assigning the magistrates with lawsuits to juries that had already been selected for the day.[16] This required the juries of any one day to be the same size.[17] In this lottery, Aristotle's pupil explains, the magistrate whose name is drawn out first goes to the lawcourt that is drawn first, the second magistrate to the second court, and *hōsautōs tois allois* ("and in like manner to the others" — 66.1). Here the treatise's author assumed that a minimum of four lawcourts sat on any one day. Thus, a cautious estimate of the average number of jurors who judged lawsuits each day in the later fourth century would be 1,604. At 3 ob. per day for 200 sitting days, their combined wages would have added up to 26 t. 4,400 dr. per year.[18] As the democracy presumably handled just as much legal business forty years earlier, this cost estimate also stands for the 370s.

In the 420s the number of legal cases that the Athenian law-courts heard would have been considerably higher. In large part this was a result of demography ([Xen.] *Ath. Pol.* 3.6): since the population of Athens was probably twice as large as it would be in the fourth century, there were simply more wrongdoers and more citizens willing to pursue them in a lawcourt. But it was also due to the *arkhē*.[19] In the 450s and the 440s Athens intervened in the legal affairs of only those cities that it had forced back into the *arkhē* after a revolt.[20] With Erythrae, for example, the Athenian *dēmos* decreed that this city could not exile a citizen without its consent (*IG* i³ 14.26–29), while it gave any citizen of Chalcis who had been convicted there of a crime whose punishment was *atimia* ("loss of citizenship rights"), exile, or death the right to lodge a legal appeal at Athens (40.70–76). By the late fifth century, however, all the empire's cities were prevented from judging their own citizens for crimes that carried these most serious penalties (e.g., Antiph. 5.47; Chamaeleon fr. 44 Wehrli). They could now initiate such cases only before an Athenian jury. This policy of compulsorily transferring lawsuits, which must have significantly increased the volume of legal business at Athens, was introduced, it appears, before the mid 420s, for Pseudo-Xenophon, whose own *Constitution of the Athenians* dates to this point, argued that the Athenian *dēmos* forced its subjects to conduct their lawsuits before them so that it could protect the supporters of its empire among them (1.16–18).[21]

The resulting busyness of the Athenian lawcourts of the later fifth century was reflected in different ways. The first was "the sheer prevalence of lawcourt jokes" in the period's comedies, whose basis, in most cases, was that the judging of legal *agōnes* ("contests") was the quintessential feature of the Athenians (e.g., Ar. *Av.* 32–41, 109–111, *Nub.* 206–220, *Pax* 505).[22] It was apparent too in the constraints on capacity that the legal system had hit: although Athens constantly had many courts in session at the same time (Ar. *Vesp.* 1007–1008; [Xen.] *Ath. Pol.* 3.7), it still took a long time for legal cases to be heard ([Xen.] *Ath. Pol.* 3.2–8).[23] A result of this heavy load of cases was that it was relatively easy for the year's 6,000 jurors, whenever they wished, to get on a jury.

Our sources begin to make an issue of jurors competing with each other for a spot only in the early 380s (e.g., Ar. *Plut.* 1166–1167). All of this suggests that the lawcourts of the 420s handled no less than twice as many legal cases as those of the 370s and the 330s.[24] Thus, we can safely estimate that annual jury pay cost to Athens in this decade was 53 t. 2,800 dr.

COUNCILORS

Towards the end of 412/1 oligarchs at Athens successfully intimidated the *dēmos* into suspending the democracy (Thuc. 8.63.3–69.4). Once the *boulē* ("council") of four hundred, which they had proposed, had been assembled, it forcefully ousted the democratic council of five hundred, which still had a month of its year to serve ([Arist.] *Ath. Pol.* 32.1). The Four Hundred barged into the *bouleutērion* ("council chamber") and ordered the councilors "to take their *misthos*" and to get out (Thuc. 8.69.4). In case of resistance, they had come with daggers and 120 youths as muscle. As the democratic *bouleutai* ("councilors") meekly filed out, they were handed pay "for all (*pantos*) of the rest of their term." The new council's members, by contrast, were paid at the rate of only 3 ob. per day, when it was their turn to be its *prutaneis* or executive committee ([Arist.] *Ath. Pol.* 29.5).

This infamous episode provides important evidence for the remuneration of the democracy's regular *bouleutai*. Pay for jurors was introduced in the middle of the fifth century, while magistrates were certainly receiving pay by 432/1 or a little later (see "Magistrates," below). Thus, it is most likely that Athens began to pay its *bouleutai* in the third quarter of the fifth century. There is, to be sure, implicit evidence that they were being paid in 421/0 at the latest (*IG* i³ 82.17–23).[25] But the first explicit statement that this was so comes from Thucydides' narrating of this episode. His account also gives us an insight into how councilors were paid. As the *bouleutai* of 412/1 had been remunerated up to the day of their ouster, they were evidently paid day by day, which explains why Thucydides, with his emphatic "*pantos*," drew attention to the extra inducement that the oligarchs were offering them to go quietly: a lump sum for every day in their term's balance, even though they would not be attending meetings (8.69.4).[26] In this regular system of remuneration, *bouleutai* were not paid for days when they were absent or the council did not meet.[27] This episode furnishes, finally, the only pay rate for any Athenian councilors of the fifth century.

The Athenians probably remunerated council members at different pay rates in the 420s, the 370s, and the 330s. In the later fourth century, *bouleutai* were each paid 5 ob. per day and 1 ob. extra, when they served as the council's executive committee ([Arist.] *Ath. Pol.* 62.2). The fifty councilors from each tribe on the council were *prutaneis* for one-tenth of the year (43.2).[28] During this so-called prytany, they were responsible, among other duties, for convening the meetings of the council and the assembly and drafting their agendas (43.3–4). Two-thirds of them each served as the *epistatēs* ("supervisor") of the executive committee for one whole day (44.1). He was the custodian of the state's public seal and the keys to its treasuries and, along with a third of his fellow *prutaneis*, was required to remain constantly in the headquarters of the presidents. In view of such responsibilities, every *bouleutēs* presumably turned up every day for service during his tribe's prytany (Pl. *Leg.* 758b).[29] To do so, those who lived too far from the city to walk back and forth each day would have been forced to find short-term accommodation in the *astu* ("urban center"). In addition, Athens of the later fourth century paid the executive committee 20 percent more than regular *bouleutai* to cover the meals that they took together ([Arist.] *Ath. Pol.* 62.2).

The short-lived oligarchy of 411/0 suspended *misthophoria* ("receipt of pay") for all magistrates, except the nine archons and the executive committee of its new council, as part of its efforts to redirect as much public money as possible to the armed forces ([Arist.] *Ath. Pol.* 29.4, 30.2; Thuc. 8.65.3, 8.67.3).[30] Even before it came to power, the *dēmos* had already been cutting public spending, including the pay of its sailors and soldiers, in response to the budgetary crisis that followed its serious defeat in Sicily (e.g., Thuc. 8.1.3).[31] In 411/0 Athenian oligarchs were no doubt strongly opposed to *misthophoria* on ideological grounds as well (cf. [Xen.] *Ath. Pol.* 1.13). In this context it is unlikely that what the Four Hundred paid each of their *prutaneis* was greater than—or even the same as—the regular daily pay rate for a *bouleutēs* in the later fifth century.[32] Thus, we can use their 3 ob. per day as a safe minimum for calculating the cost of council pay in the 420s. The Athenian people, no doubt, quickly restored *misthos* for councilors, as they certainly did for jurors, when they regained power at the century's close.[33] No source tells us how much *bouleutai* were paid in the 370s. As it would have been more than what the Four Hundred paid and was possibly less than the attested pay rate for the 330s, a good guess would be 4 ob. per day.

How many of the councilors who were not *prutaneis* normally attended council meetings? The council of five hundred met on no less than 275 days per year.[34] The only days on which it did not meet were *hēmerai apophrades* and those on which one of the city's yearly *heortē* was celebrated (e.g., [Arist.] *Ath. Pol.* 43.3; Dem. 24. 47–48).[35] Even on assembly days the executive committee convened a meeting of the council, when the assemblygoers had departed (e.g., Aeschin. 1.110–112). Clearly some *bouleutai* would have struggled to have turned up for so many meetings, even if they usually went for only less than half a day. This was especially the case for poor citizens who lived too far from the *astu* to walk back home before nightfall.[36] Their regular attendance in the *bouleutērion* for more than their tribe's prytany would have hampered their ability to keep their regular livelihoods going. As they did not have, as the wealthy did (e.g., Aeschin. 1.97; Isae. 11.40–43; Lys. 20.11–12), second homes in the city or its port, it would have also compelled them to search for accommodation away from home for which they would often have had to pay.[37]

A prosecution speech that Demosthenes was hired to write in 355/4 implies that absenteeism among *bouleutai* was common; for in it he claimed that ordinary council members did not make speeches, propose resolutions, "or even perhaps go for the most part to the *bouleutērion*" (22.36). Against this we must weigh three factors that encouraged *bouleutai* to attend regularly. In the same speech, firstly, Demosthenes provided evidence of the fact that Athenians were proud of their service as councilors (e.g., 10, 35).[38] The democracy, secondly, facilitated their participation by not only paying them but also exempting them from military service during their year on the council (Lycurg. 1.37). Classical Athenians, finally, were under "some group pressure" to take political participation seriously (e.g., Ar. *Plut.* 185–188, 307–310; Thuc. 2.40.2).[39]

Weighing these different factors, I believe that Hansen's estimate of how many *bouleutai* normally participated seems plausible: in addition to the fifty *prutaneis* who were on duty every day of the year, two-thirds of the other councilors turned up at the council's 275 meetings per year.[40] At the pay rates that are attested for the 330s, this level of participation would have cost the Athenians 14 t. 3,000 dr. per year.[41] We probably should assume that the council's executive committee had always received 20 percent more than the other councilors. On the basis of the other pay rates for which I have argued, this assumption would mean that the same level of participation on the part of *bouleutai* would have cost 9 t. 4,625 dr. in the 420s and 11 t. 3,600 dr. in the 370s.

ASSEMBLYGOERS

The Athenians introduced assembly pay considerably later than the other forms of remuneration for political participation. In the later fifth century they used the threat of a monetary penalty, not the paying of *misthos*, to ensure that enough citizens attended assembly meetings on the hill of the Pnyx (figure 3.1).[42] Before each meeting, citizens who were loitering in the marketplace were moved to the Pnyx by a row of Scythian archers holding a red-dyed rope (e.g., Ar. *Ach.* 20–22; Poll. 8.114). Any citizen with a red stain on his clothes who was not at the meeting was fined. Immediately after the democracy's restoration in 404/3, the presidents tried many comparable techniques "to bring the crowd near for ratification of the voting" ([Arist.] *Ath. Pol.* 41.3). As they consistently failed to get the required quorum for ratification, the *dēmos* supported Agyrrhius' proposal to start paying assemblygoers

FIGURE 3.1.
View of the meeting place of the assembly, directly above the Athenian
agora *on the hill of the Pnyx. Photograph courtesy of the American School*
of Classical Studies at Athens, Alison Frantz Photographic Collection.

1 ob. per meeting (Ar. *Eccl.* 184–186).[43] When even this did not
make citizens move from the *agora* ("marketplace") to the Pnyx
(300–301), Heraclides convinced the Athenians to raise assembly
pay to 2 ob., while Agyrrhius quickly got it raised again to 3 ob.
([Arist.] *Ath. Pol.* 41.3).

The availability of pay at the last rate, which is first attested in a
comedy of the late 390s (e.g., Ar. *Eccl.* 289–291, 307–310), attracted
more than enough assemblygoers to run meetings (e.g., Ar. *Plut.*
171, 328–330).[44] It made it considerably easier too for meetings to
start on time.[45] By the 330s assemblygoers were each paid 1 dr.
3 ob. for attending a *kuria ekklēsia* ("sovereign assembly"), which
was the main assembly meeting of each prytany, and 1 dr. for
the other meetings ([Arist.] *Ath. Pol.* 62.2). In the course of the
century, then, there was a massive increase in what Athens paid

assemblygoers.[46] As Agyrrhius' second rate probably continued to attract good numbers for some time, it is more likely that this increase occurred in the century's second half, when, we know, the city's public income was steadily increasing.[47] Thus, I use the rate of 3 ob. per meeting for costing this form of remuneration in the 370s.

In the fourth century the Athenians competed among themselves for assembly pay, as they did for jury pay. In *Wealth* Aristophanes notes how "for the sake of 3 ob. we jostle with each other in the assembly" (329–330). Some who turned up for an assembly meeting missed out on *misthos* altogether (e.g., Ar. *Eccl.* 187). Citizens were more likely to miss getting paid the later they arrived on the Pnyx (282–284, 289–291, 380–383). All of this suggests that the Athenians did not pay more citizens for attending than was required to have a quorum.[48] Each citizen arriving before the quorum's formation received a *sumbolon* or token (295), which he exchanged, no doubt, for his pay at the close of the assembly meeting.[49] A quorum of 6,000 was required when the assembly voted on matters concerning the citizenship rights of individuals (e.g., Andoc. 1.87; Dem. 24.45–46). In particular there was a law that the vote that was taken at one assembly meeting to grant a foreigner citizenship had to be ratified at the next meeting by a secret ballot of not less than 6,000 assemblygoers ([Dem.] 59.89–90; *IG* ii² 102).[50] As the *dēmos* made hundreds of foreigners citizens in the fourth century, such ballots were, unsurprisingly, a regular part of assembly meetings.[51] Because there needed to be 6,000 or more present to hold them, Hansen is surely right to infer that this was the figure that the Athenians set as the quorum for their assemblies.[52]

In Aristotle's day there were one sovereign assembly and three other assembly meetings in each prytany ([Arist.] *Ath. Pol.* 43.3–4). In the 370s the assembly certainly met no less than forty times per year.[53] During the Peloponnesian War it probably met just as often, given the amount of foreign policy on which the *dēmos* had to deliberate.[54] At forty meetings per year, the annual cost of pay for 6,000 assemblygoers was 20 t. in the 370s.[55] At the higher rates that Athens paid in the 330s assembly pay added up to 45 t. per year.[56]

MAGISTRATES

In his treatise's first half, which charts the historical development of the Athenian constitution, Aristotle's pupil gave figures for how many magistrates Athens had employed in the fifth century. After completing the Delian League's first tribute assessment in 478/7, Aristides, he wrote, advised the Athenians to seize the league's leadership and to migrate from Attica to the *astu*, where everyone would earn pay by soldiering, carrying out guard duty, or participating in politics ([Arist.] *Ath. Pol.* 24.1).[57] The Athenians, it is claimed, accepted his advice and hence used imperial income to pay "more than 20,000 men" (3). Among those in the fourteen different groups whom the treatise's author identified as recipients of this pay were 6,000 jurors, 1,600 archers, 1,200 horsemen, and "internal magistrates up to 700 men (*eis heptakosious andras*) and overseas magistrates up to 700 (*eis heptakosious*)."

Doubts have long been raised about the last two figures. Because the creation of new *arkhai* or magistracies and the abolition of old ones apparently canceled each other out in classical Athens, there was more or less the same number of them at home in both centuries.[58] In the second half of his treatise, however, which analyzes the constitution of the later fourth century, Aristotle's pupil mentions only 329 *arkhai*.[59] Some scholars have assumed that his account of the magistracies of his own day was "fairly exhaustive" and hence concluded that it refutes his two earlier figures for *arkhai*, which, it has been suggested, were corrupted in the treatise's transmission over the centuries.[60] Others have simply thought the repetition of "*eis heptakosious*" at 24.3 suspicious and hence put it down to a scribe who mistakenly copied 700 twice.[61] The treatise's editors have consistently treated this second figure as a corruption.

As evidence for the early fifth century, this chapter in the *Con-*

stitution of the Athenians is manifestly unreliable. The Athenians moved all together to the *astu* for the first time only during the Peloponnesian War's first phase in response to the annual invasions of Attica by Sparta (Thuc. 1.143.4–5; [Xen.] *Ath. Pol.* 2.16).[62] We know too that they increased the size of their cavalry to 1,200 members only in the later 440s or the early 430s.[63] By the mid-420s the Athenian *dēmos* was giving its magistrates *misthos* ([Xen.] *Ath. Pol.* 1.13; cf. [Arist.] *Ath. Pol.* 29.5; *IG* i³ 82.17–23), but the earliest explicit evidence for it is a decree that is now dated to 432/1 or a little later (*IG* i³ 32.8–9).[64] Certainly this form of remuneration was not introduced before jury pay was in the 450s (see "Jurors," above). Thus, it was blatantly anachronistic for Aristotle's pupil to associate these particular developments with Aristides, whose political career came to an end in the mid-470s.[65]

Yet his chapter does convey some reliable information about the later fifth century, for contemporary sources confirm that during this period Athens did, for example, choose 6,000 citizens every year as jurors (Ar. *Vesp.* 660–663) and have archery and cavalry corps of 1,600 and 1,200 respectively (Thuc. 2.13.8). Indeed his chapter parallels what we find in comedies from the Peloponnesian War: Aristophanes for one made a comparable proposal for the empire's subjects to support 20,000 Athenians (*Vesp.* 701–711), while Eupolis, one of his comic rivals, linked Aristides and three other dead politicians with a time when Athens was better led (Eup. fr. 99.35–39, 78–120; 105 Kassel and Austin). Thus, much of this chapter's content may be based on a lost work of old comedy.[66]

More than thirty years ago Hansen proved the reliability of the figure that Aristotle's pupil gave for internal magistracies.[67] The pupil's account of the constitution of his own day turns out to have been far from exhaustive: although it refers to 329 magistrates, other literary sources, along with inscriptions, show that there were another 129 *arkhontes* that it simply fails to mention.[68] Hansen plausibly argues that the Athenians had even more magistrates than our patchy sources indicate.[69] In particular they must have appointed supervisory boards for the few dozen cults of Attica whose management the democracy took over in the fifth century.[70] As only a few of them recorded their accounts on stone, in most cases we lack direct evidence of their existence. Thus, for the sake of managing their countryside's festivals and sanctuaries effectively, the Athenians, Hansen suggests, appointed up to another 200 *arkhontes*, which brings the total of their magistrates to 658.[71] As their numbers remained relatively stable throughout the classical period, this tally ends up confirming the "up to 700 men" that the *Constitution of the Athenians* gave for internal magistrates in the fifth century.

What we know of the *arkhē* of the later fifth century corroborates that Athens employed, in this period at least, the same number of citizens as overseas magistrates (e.g., [Xen.] *Ath. Pol.* 1.19; cf. RO 22.22–23). At this time Athens had, it seems, magistrates in most of the *poleis* ("city-states") that it ruled. A decree on tribute, for example, which is now dated to the 420s, made its collection the responsibility of the Athenian democratic council, *episkopoi* ("inspectors") and *arkhontes* in the cities (*IG* i³ 34.6–11).[72] Athenian *episkopoi* visited a city for only a short period to find out what it was doing or to oversee, for example, the establishment of a democracy that Athens was imposing (e.g., Ar. *Av.* 1020–1034; *IG* i³ 14.13–15).[73] By contrast, *arkhontes* were based in a city year round. Also in the 420s the Athenian *dēmos* passed a decree that made it compulsory for its subjects to use its coins, measures and weights (*IG* i³ 1453). This decree may have recognized that not every *polis* ("city-state") hosted Athenian magistrates (4.1–2), but it still made them primarily responsible for its enactment (3.1–2, 8.1–2). Both decrees would not have given them the responsibilities that they did unless these magistrates were present in most of the empire's states.[74]

This Athenian presence consisted of boards instead of individual magistrates. This has certainly been recognized in relation to *poleis* that had attempted unsuccessfully to abandon the *arkhē*.[75] Athens sent such boards to, for example, Erythrae, Miletus, and Samos after it had crushed their revolts (e.g., Thuc. 1.115.1–3; *IG* i³ 14.13–15; i³ 21.5–7, 39, 45). Nevertheless, it was also clearly the case for every city that had imperial officials (e.g., *IG* i³ 62.5–7, 281.66–68, 282.11–14). In his *Birds*, for example, Aristophanes made out that the Athenians normally sent a city "inspectors" or "magistrates" (1032–1034, 1050), while the so-called coinage decree assumed the same (e.g., *IG* i³ 1453, B/G, 8.1–2). This giving of magistracies to groups, not individuals, was, of course, a standard practice of Athenian democracy.[76] As the empire had around 175 subject city-states during the Peloponnesian War's first phase, the presence of multiple *arkhontes* in a majority suggests that the "up to 700" overseas magistrates in the *Constitution of the Athenians* was actually based on genuine evidence from the later fifth century.[77] It may not be what is expected but Athens probably had the same number of overseas *arkhontes* as it had internal magistrates in the 420s.[78]

Hansen argues that the democracy did not give magistrates *misthos* in the fourth century. He founds his argument on the silence of our ancient sources.[79] The Four Hundred made magistrates, excepting the nine archons, *amisthoi* or unsalaried ([Arist.] *Ath. Pol.* 29.5; cf. Thuc. 8.65.3, 8.67.3), and if, after their ouster, this form of remuneration was restored, it was once more taken away by the oligarchic regime of 405/4.[80] For Hansen no evidence exists that the democracy either in the following year, that is, after its second restoration, or at any other point in the fourth century started paying all of its magistrates again. In his account of the 320s Aristotle's pupil noted the remuneration of only a fraction of the 329 *arkhontes* that he got around to describing. They were the nine archons, five magistrates who were based overseas, and ten others who managed the state's new training program for ephebes (42.3; 62.2). On *misthos*, at least, Hansen thinks that the *Constitution of the Athenians* is not "ridiculously incomplete" and is corroborated by the silence of the century's inscriptions on *misthophoria* for magistrates (cf. *IG* ii² 145.9–10; RO 58.5–12).[81] Thus, its very short list of salaried officials suggests that the Athenians never reversed what the oligarchs had done. The democracy they restored was more conservative than the fifth-century one.[82] Hansen concludes: "Considerable concessions were made to the oligarchic criticism of radical democracy and the principle 'no *misthos* for *archai*' may well have been one of those concessions."[83]

In almost all cases, fourth-century magistrates may have no

longer received *misthos*, but Hansen thinks that many of them still found other forms of compensation.[84] Certainly the state gave some of its religious officials a share, for example, of the animals they sacrificed, produce from a sanctuary's lands, or free meals in the lead-up to a festival.[85] Hansen argues that magistrates also relied on their own initiative to get compensation: some demanded cash gifts from those requiring their help, while others held onto public funds and used them privately for years.[86] Generals too, he argues, pocketed large gifts from foreigners and most of the booty they had captured.[87] For Hansen, a magistrate's taking of such benefits was common and generally accepted by the *dēmos*.[88] But if a magistrate's requests or acts went beyond "the accepted limits," he could be prosecuted for taking bribes or misappropriating funds. In three of his treatises Isocrates discussed the money that Athenians earned apparently as magistrates (7.24–27, 12.145, 15.145–152). In two of them, Hansen argues, he had in mind only the benefits that *arkhontes* secured independently, while in the third the reference is instead to pay for a different form of political participation.[89]

The initial reception of Hansen's position on pay for postwar magistrates was mixed. P. J. Rhodes rejected it immediately.[90] Vincent Gabrielsen published a critique of it as a book.[91] Admittedly some did quickly back up Hansen but just as many did not.[92] To this day, ancient historians take different sides in this debate.[93] Thus, it is simply *not* the case that Hansen's position is widely accepted.[94] I believe there to be three reasons why his position should be questioned.[95] The first reason is that the *dēmos* simply did not tolerate any misuse of an archonship for personal gain. This makes unlikely the common accepting of bribes and stealing of public funds that Hansen proposes. The second reason is that poor Athenians served as magistrates. Citizens of this social class had to earn a living. Since many of the *arkhai* that they filled were full time, they could not have done so unless they received compensation for lost earnings. Legally this could come only as *misthos* from the state.

The third reason is evidence. Hansen's treatment of the treatise of Aristotle's pupil is inconsistent: here he argues that it is not seriously incomplete, but, when it came to the number of magistrates, he argued just the opposite (see above). More serious is that we do have evidence for the state's payment of fourth-century officials and lack evidence for what we should see if Hansen were right. In costing Athenian democracy my book relies heavily on Hansen's important quantification of the democracy's activity and the participation of its citizens.[96] Certainly his lifetime's work has transformed our understanding of Athenian democracy. On the remuneration of magistrates, however, we should not follow him. *Misthos* for them was probably reintroduced at the same time as it was for councilors and jurors, that is, immediately after the democracy's second restoration in 404/3.

Athenians of the fourth century had a very negative view of magistrates who took bribes or misappropriated public funds.[97] For them this behavior was "terrible and abominable" (Antiph. 6.49). Public speakers consistently described such acts as *adikēmata* or wrongs (e.g., Antiph. 6.35, 49, 2.1.6; Dem. 24.5, 102, 110–111; Lys. 27.4, 6). The *dēmos* believed that bribes corrupted magistrates (e.g., Lys. 28.9; 30.2, 5, 25). In no way were accepting them and stealing public money thought of as norms.[98] "Just" or "good" magistrates committed neither crime (Lys. 28.9, 15–16).[99] The nine archons vowed not "to take *dōra* ('gifts') on account of their magistracy" ([Arist.] *Ath. Pol.* 55.5). The *dēmos* acted on this strongly held belief. They made it illegal for a magistrate to take gifts or to steal public funds ([Arist.] *Ath. Pol.* 54.2, 59.3).[100] "Nor were the Athenian people loath to inflict severe penalties on magistrates who failed them."[101] When it came to these *graphai*, their jurors showed no leniency (e.g., Dem. 19.273, 22.39, 24.112; Lys. 28.3–4, 29.6), convicting *arkhontes*, for example, for a short delay in returning public funds or accepting small-scale bribes (Dem. 19.293). A magistrate who was convicted of either *graphē* was fined ten times what he had taken illegally (e.g., Din. 1.60; 2.17).

For the sake of catching such wrongdoers, the fourth-century democracy monitored its magistrates closely.[102] In the *kuria ekklēsia* of each prytany a vote was taken on their performance ([Arist.] *Ath. Pol.* 43.4, 61.2).[103] This was the chance for anyone to accuse a magistrate of wrongdoing (e.g., Aeschin. 1.110; [Dem.] 50.12; Dem. 58.28). Private citizens could accuse a public official of "not using the *nomoi* or laws" before the council ([Arist.] *Ath. Pol.* 45.2).[104] A *bouleutēs* could do the same (Antiph. 6.12, 35, 45, 49). Such denunciations normally ended up before a lawcourt (e.g., [Arist.] *Ath. Pol.* 45.2, 61.2). In addition, the accounts of every magistrate were regularly checked. A committee of the *boulē* did so every prytany ([Arist.] *Ath. Pol.* 45.2, 48.3; Lys. 30.5).[105] At the end of his term a magistrate also underwent an *euthuna*.[106] The mainstay of this public scrutiny was the auditing of his *logos* or accounts (e.g., [Arist.] *Ath. Pol.* 48.4-5, 54.2; Dem. 18.117, 19.273; cf. Aeschin. 3.23). He had to be present for his audit's results. They were announced before a jury of 501 so that, if evidence of malfeasance was revealed, he could be prosecuted straightaway on one or more of the *graphai* concerning magistrates (Aeschin. 3.10).

Wealthy Athenians could afford lessons in public speaking and hence found it easy to denounce a magistrate for wrongdoing on the Pnyx or in the *bouleutērion*.[107] A motivation for them doing so often was that the official whom they were accusing was a personal enemy (e.g., Antiph. 2.1.5, 6; Aeschin. 1.100; Dem. 24.8–9).[108] Thus, it is no surprise that many of the known *arkhontes* who were prosecuted were politicians.[109] It was taken for granted that poor citizens as individuals were far less capable of pursuing wrongdoers through the lawcourts (e.g., Dem. 44.28, 21.123–124, 141, 219; Lys. 24.16–17).[110] Importantly the democracy's monitoring of its officeholders relied only in part on this initiative of wealthy individuals, as the checking of accounts was in the hands of committees. In particular a board of ten *logistai* or public auditors scrutinized a magistrate's *logos* at the end of his term (Aeschin. 1.107; [Arist.] *Ath. Pol.* 54.2). If they suspected him of committing a public offense, his prosecution did not depend on their ability as public speakers, as they had the use of ten *sunēgoroi* ("public prosecutors") for this purpose.[111] The result was that poor Athenians too were regularly convicted for financial crimes that they had committed as magistrates (e.g., Lys. 27.4–6; Dem. 24.112).

This lack of tolerance that fourth-century Athens manifestly had of bribe taking and stealing public funds makes it highly unlikely that they were common practices among its 700-odd magistrates. The *dēmos* strongly believed that good officeholders did not commit such acts. Thus, *aiskhunē* or a sense of shame would have dissuaded the vast majority from engaging in such *adikēmata*.[112] Magistrates feared too the *nomoi* regulating their service. They did not need to be reminded of the constant monitoring under which they carried out their duties and the penchant of their fellow citizens for harshly punishing *arkhontes* who erred. Poor magistrates especially would have struggled to pay the fine of ten times the amount stolen that a conviction brought. The *atimia* that public debtors suffered made this penalty in itself a strong deterrent.[113]

The prosecution of *stratēgoi* ("generals") by fourth-century Athens shows how there was no level of acceptance of wrongdoing by magistrates. With the collapse of the *arkhē*, generals were regularly sent out without enough public funds to pay for their expeditions.[114] In these circumstances they made up the shortfall by drawing on the booty that they had captured (Diod. Sic. 15.47.7; Nep. *Timoth.* 1; Xen. *Hell.* 6.2.36), plundering the countryside of the enemy (Isoc. 15.111–112; Polyaen. 3.10.9), or forcing cities in or near the theater of operations to make "contributions" (Aeschin. 2.71–72; Dem. 8.24–86).[115] But they could not treat such funds as their own, as the *imperatores* of the Roman Republic would come to do.[116] Money so raised was judged to be public property.[117] The *dēmos* authorized its collection and usage either before a *stratēgos* departed or during a campaign (Dem. 8.9; Diod. Sic. 16.57.2–3; Lys. 28.5–6).[118] On his return he submitted a *logos* of what he had raised in the field and handed over any surplus to the city (Dem. 20.17–80; Lys. 28.6).[119]

In the fourth century two out of each year's ten generals were on average the targets of an *eisangelia eis ton dēmon* or denunciation before the people.[120] This prosecution was employed in cases of treason or political corruption (e.g., Dem. 49.67; Hyp. 3.7–8).[121] Almost every case involving a *stratēgos* resulted in his conviction (Dem. 19.180).[122] Understandably, *stratēgoi* feared the possibility of such a denunciation back home (e.g., Thuc. 1.49.4, 3.98.5, 7.48.4–5; Diod. Sic. 15.31.1).[123] Some of these cases centered on a general's handling of funds. In 390/89, for example, Ergocles was denounced for accepting *dōra* and stealing public funds that he had raised in the field as a general (Lys. 28.1–2, 11; 29.2, 5, 11).[124] He was condemned to death by the *dēmos* and quickly executed (29.2). In 356/5 Timotheus, who had won many victories for Athens, was denounced by a fellow general for accepting gifts from foreigners (Din. 1.14, 3.17).[125] The people fined him an unprecedented 100 t. (Isoc. 15.129; Nep. *Timoth.* 3.5). He was unable to pay and so went into exile, where he died soon afterwards (Plut. *Mor.* 605f). Such denunciations left Athenian *stratēgoi* in no doubt of the danger of any appearance of financial wrongdoing.

Poor Athenians volunteered to fill magistracies requiring a full-time commitment. Demosthenes assumed that they regularly served as, for example, *astunomoi* (24.112). This board's responsibilities were the safety and the cleanliness of the streets (e.g., *IG* ii² 380).[126] Five of its members worked in Athens and five in its port ([Arist.] *Ath. Pol.* 50.2). Aristotle's pupil writes: "They prevent buildings which encroach on the streets, balconies which extend over the streets, overhead drain pipes which discharge on the streets, and window-shutters which open into the street."[127] In addition, the *astunomoi* forced the city's dung collectors to dump their loads well beyond its walls and removed the bodies of the dead homeless. They enforced, finally, the *nomoi* that the Athenians passed occasionally against the elite's conspicuous consumption (e.g., Diog. Laert. 6.90).[128] Fulfilling these demanding duties would have required every member of this board to work on a full-time basis.

There is direct evidence of poor citizens also serving as *agoranomoi* (Dem. 24.112), treasurers of Athena ([Arist.] *Ath. Pol.* 47.1), and the *basileus* or king ([Dem.] 39.72). What we know of these *arkhontes* indicates that their duties were no less time consuming.[129] Indeed 42 of the 87 magistracies that Athens had in the 320s probably required a full-time commitment (see Table 3.1 below). As poor citizens commonly were magistrates (e.g., Dem. *Exordia* 55; Lys. 24.9, 13; 27.4–5), many of them would have filled these more demanding roles.[130] In doing so they had to neglect other daytime commitments. We have seen how poor Athenians had to work for a living.[131] Consequently they could not have taken up full-time magistracies unless they were compensated for lost earnings.[132] Because *nomoi* stopped magistrates from securing it on their own initiative, this compensation could come legally only as *misthos* from the state.

Three treatises of Isocrates give evidence of the continuation of the democracy's payment of its *arkhontes* into the fourth century.[133] This writer composed his *Areopagiticus* and *Panathenaicus* mid-century.[134] In them he argued that the Athenians should replace the form of the democracy to which theirs had degenerated with the form that, he claimed, it had originally taken (e.g., 7.15–19, 15.145–152). In support of what was in fact an argument for the disempowerment of the *dēmos*, Isocrates contrasted this ancestral constitution's magistrates with those of his day (7.22–27, 15.145–147).[135] Every one of the ancestral magistrates, he writes, was elected and, instead of receiving *misthos*, often had to spend his own money (7.22, 24–25; 15.145). Consequently they were motivated out of a sense of duty (7.24). Because these *arkhai* were the same as the liturgies that wealthy citizens of the classical period were required to perform (12.145), most archaic Athenians avoided them (7.25, 12.146).[136]

By contrast, fourth-century *arkhontes* were appointed by lot and paid (7.22–24, 15.145–146). For Isocrates their only motive was personal gain (7.25). Indeed he characterized them as thoroughly money-grubbing: they knew "more accurately the *prosodoi* or incomes from the magistracies than from their own businesses" (7.24), while, when they took up their positions, their first act was to see whether their predecessors had overlooked any *lemma* ("payment") to which they had been entitled (25).[137] With money to be made, there was now intense competition for *arkhai* (7.24–25, 15.145). Isocrates confirmed, finally, that this pay came from only the state, for he wrote of how the ancestral magistrates, in contrast to contemporary ones, did not "keep house out of public funds" and abstained completely from "the money of the *polis*" (7.24–25).

In these treatises Isocrates was obviously expressing the negative view of what motivated hundreds of poor Athenians to serve as *arkhontes* every year.[138] He was able to do so, because he was writing for only elite readers.[139] They generally had criticisms of the contemporary democracy and expected the intellectuals whom they targeted to address them.[140] Consequently Isocrates was free to articulate their criticisms and to advocate strongly for constitutional changes. Nonetheless, other aspects of his depiction of magistrates are corroborated by his contemporaries. In a legal speech Lysias, for one, noted how magistrates were paid out of public funds (21.19; cf. 19.56–57). Certainly fourth-century writers give the impression that Athenians competed fiercely for *arkhai*.[141] In most cases they were referring to the one hundred or so of them that were filled by election.[142] There apparently, however, was competition too for the other magistracies: a lottery was normally required to appoint them (e.g., Dem. 39.102; Lys. 6.4, 31.33), which suggests that the volunteers who had offered themselves for offices exceeded the number of positions available.

This testimony of Isocrates is bolstered by what we do *not* see in the fourth century's legal speeches.[143] Without *misthos*, Athenian magistracies would—as Isocrates suggested—have resembled liturgies, because they would have been a burden on those who held them. Wealthy defendants invariably sought to win over juries by cataloguing the liturgies and other *agatha* or public benefactions that they had undertaken for the city (e.g., Lys. 3.46, 12.38, 30.1).[144] Some even admitted that they had performed such benefactions only to secure the *kharis* or gratitude of any future jury (e.g., Lys. 18.23, 20.31, 25.11–13). Thus, if *arkhai* were unsalaried and so akin to liturgies, we should find speakers regularly discussing them in court. But this is exactly what we do not find: elite litigants simply did not list magistracies among their public benefactions.[145]

In his *Antidosis* Isocrates actually made a virtue out of his lack of experience as a magistrate. In the mid-350s he was challenged to an *antidosis* or an exchange of properties.[146] A citizen who had been assigned a trierarchy believed that Isocrates was better qualified to carry it out because of his apparently greater wealth. Consequently he used the *antidosis* procedure to challenge him either to take over this liturgy or to exchange properties with him.[147] Isocrates refused to do either, and so it fell to a jury to work out who should bear this liturgy. This case, which he lost (12.5–6, 144–

145), showed him clearly how many Athenians viewed very nega-
tively his métier as a teacher of public speaking and his relationship to their democracy more generally (4–5). Isocrates claimed
that this third treatise was his attempt to rehabilitate his public
image (7–10). In it Isocrates portrayed himself as a benefactor by
asserting repeatedly that he preferred to perform *agatha* than to
hold paid positions (e.g., 150–151). In Chapter 145, for example, he
wrote how he had refrained from "the *arkhai* and the profits that
are there and all other *koinōn* or public prerogatives." Yet this did
not stop him performing liturgies. Isocrates, finally, confirmed
again that the state paid magistrates when, in Chapter 152, he explained why he had always avoided "the *lēmmata* or payments
from the city." Because Isocrates was claiming that he had never
accepted political pay during his life, this treatise, which he wrote
in his eighties, actually serves as evidence of the remuneration
of Athenian magistrates throughout the first half of the fourth
century.[148]

Hansen's position on the manner in which magistrates received their *misthos*, when, that is, they happened to be paid, is
also open to question. Unfortunately, there is no evidence on how
classical Athens remunerated its *arkhontes*. In the face of this
silence, Hansen assumes that they were paid in the same way as
jurors, councilors, and assemblygoers,[149] who were paid for only
the actual days on which they performed their duties.[150] We know
too that they were handed their *misthos* at the close of the lawcourt's, council's, or assembly's business for the day. For Hansen,
magistrates were remunerated only at the conclusion of each day
on which they met with other members of their board or otherwise carried out their duties. He does not believe that they were
paid for every day of the year.

I believe that this means of remuneration was unlikely for
two reasons. Firstly, it is hard to see how what Hansen proposes
could have been put into effect. In the later fifth century it was
the *kōlakretai* ("ham collectors") who were mainly responsible
for handing out the different forms of remuneration for public
service. At this time they were the state's main spending magistrates.[151] We find them giving *misthos* to, for example, the *epistatai*

("supervisors") of the Eleusinian sanctuary (*IG* i³ 32.8–9), *hiero-poioi* ("doers of sacred things") for the Hephaesteia (82.21–22), jurors (Ar. *Vesp.* 694), heralds (*IG* i³ 71.50–51), and the priestess of Athena Nike (*IG* i³ 30.8–9).[152] Certainly individual ham collectors could have turned up at the *bouleutērion* and at each lawcourt, before they were closed for the day, with the pay for those councilors and jurors who were present, but it would have been impossible for them to pay magistrates on the same daily basis. Athens had up to 87 different magistracies and appointed up to 658 internal magistrates each year. The *kōlakretai*, along with the officials who took over their duties in the fourth century, simply could not have kept track of so many *arkhontes*.[153] Since such officials did not know the days on which each and every board conducted business and which of its members were present, they were simply in no position to employ the method of remuneration that they used for jurors, councilors and assemblygoers.

The second reason for questioning Hansen's position relates to how public servants were paid in classical Athens. These state employees worked alongside magistrates or, at least, had regular contact with them. Therefore, we can reasonably assume that they were probably remunerated in the same manner as magistrates. Thus, if what Hansen proposes is correct, there should be evidence of these public servants being paid only on the days when they actually worked. This, however, is not what we find. The accounts, for example, of the Eleusinian sanctuary for, possibly, 333/2 detail the daily pay rates of those who were employed on building works there and the total amounts that they were paid for the entire year (*IG* ii² 1673.57–62).[154] The sanctuary's *epistatai*, they tell us, paid an elected architect 2 dr. per day, an elected scribe 3 ob., and the *epistatēs* or supervisor of the public slaves 1⅔ ob. When the amounts they received for the year are divided by these daily pay rates, these public servants, it emerges, were paid for every day of the year, even though they would have stopped work during, for instance, the Eleusinian Mysteries and other yearly *heortai*. The accounts of 329/8 recorded only amounts that personnel were paid prytany by prytany (*IG* ii² 1672.5–6, 11–12, 43–44, 118–119, 142–143).[155] But when these sums are averaged out over the prytany's number of days, we find the same elected architect receiving 2 dr. per day; an elected scribe, 1 ob.; and a supervisor of the public slaves, 1⅔ ob. The similarities with the pay rates of the early accounts indicate that the sanctuary's employees were again paid for every day of the year.

The building accounts of the Erechtheum tell the same story. Those of 408/7 recorded lump sums that were paid to an architect and a *hupogrammateus* or undersecretary (*IG* i³ 476.59–60, 266–268).[156] When these sums are divided by each prytany's days, we see that the architect was paid 1 dr. for every single day and the undersecretary, 5 ob. Like public servants, magistrates were most probably remunerated at a fixed daily pay rate for every day of the year in which they served.[157] This was the only practical means for the *kōlakretai* to pay such a large number of individuals. By analogy with what we see in the accounts above, they possibly handed out *misthos* to internal *arkhontes* as lump sums once every prytany.

There is limited direct evidence for how much Athens paid its magistrates in the later fourth century. The *Constitution of the Athenians* from the 320s notes only how the nine archons were each paid 4 ob. per day (62.2), while the *sōphronistai*, who commanded the ephebes of their respective tribes, the archon on Salamis, and the Delian amphictyons each took 1 dr. per day (42.3; 62.2). As limited as this evidence is, it suggests, at least, that the Athenian democracy paid its magistrates at different daily pay rates. This is corroborated by accounts that we have just considered, because they record state employees earning different amounts of pay for work on the same building projects.

It has been widely assumed that the more time an Athenian magistrate spent performing his duties, the higher his daily pay rate was.[158] I too think it likely that a proportional relationship existed between the time a position took up and the payment of the *misthos* that it customarily attracted. Because they presided over the lawcourts and had other heavy religious or administrative duties (e.g., [Arist.] *Ath. Pol.* 55–59; Ar. *Eccl.* 289–291), the nine archons clearly had little free time during their annual terms.[159] Thus, the 4 ob. they earned can be taken as the standard rate that

Athens paid *arkhontes* who served on a full-time basis. Because the *sōphronistai* and probably the archon on Salamis needed every working day to carry out their duties (e.g., [Arist.] *Ath. Pol.* 42.2–5), it would appear that Athens paid an extra 2 ob. per day to full-time magistrates who were part of the armed forces or based overseas. This higher rate was the standard one that Athens of the later fifth and fourth centuries paid its soldiers and sailors when they were on campaign.[160]

We may not know the pay rates of the vast majority of magistrates in the later fourth century, but the period's inscriptions, in combination with the treatise of Aristotle's pupil, do, at least, clarify what their duties were.[161] On the basis of this evidence, it is possible to estimate roughly whether a post required a full-time, half-time, or quarter-time commitment from its holders. Such an estimate can be combined with one or the other of the standard full-time rates to produce a daily pay rate for each magistracy.[162] Table 3.1 gives the results of this estimating. It lists the up-to-87 magistracies that Athens of the later fourth century had, in the order in which they are discussed in the *Constitution of the Athenians* and, after that, in Hansen's analysis of those that this treatise fails to mention.[163] No rates are recorded for the amphictyons and the treasurers of the city's so-called sacred triremes, because Athens did not pay them: Delos directly paid these representatives of Athens ([Arist.] *Ath. Pol.* 62.2), while the treasurer positions for the *Paralus* and the *Ammon* were, in fact, liturgies, as their holders were expected to pay the expenses that trierarchs normally bore.[164] As the number of people, finally, who held each magistracy is known, these daily pay rates can be used to calculate what was the annual cost of employing 658 *arkhontes*. In the 330s the total of the *misthos* that Athens paid its officials was 29 t. 3,025 dr. per year.[165]

In 432/1 or a little earlier the Athenian *dēmos* created the Eleusinian *epistatai* whose accounts we have from the later fourth century.[166] The decree that brought this board into being states that its members "will receive 4 ob. each from the *kōlakretai*" (*IG* i³ 32.8–9). This happens to be the only other securely attested daily pay rate for a magistrate in classical Athens.[167] This new board's

TABLE 3.1. NUMBERS AND DAILY PAY RATES OF MAGISTRATES IN THE 330S

No.	Magistrate	Pay	No.	Magistrate	Pay
10	sōphronistai	1 dr.	1	polemarkhos	4 ob.
1	kosmētēs	1 dr.	6	thesmothetai	4 ob.
1	tamiai stratiōtikōn	4 ob.	10	athlothetai	1 ob.
10	hoi epi to theōrikon	4 ob.	10	stratēgoi	1 dr.
1	ho tōn krēnōn epimelētēs	4 ob.	10	taxiarkhoi	1 dr.
10	tamias tēs Athēnas	4 ob.	2	hipparkhoi	1 dr.
10	pōlētai	4 ob.	10	phularkhoi	1 dr.
10	apodektai	1 ob.	1	hipparkhos eis Lēmnon	1 dr.
10	katalogeis	1 ob.	1	tamias tēs Paralou	0
1	tamias tois adunatois	4 ob.	1	tamias tēs Ammōnos	0
10	hierōn episkeuastai	2 ob.	5	amphiktuones eis Dēlian	0
10	astunomoi	4 ob.	1	anagrapheus	4 ob.
10	agoranomoi	4 ob.	1	antigrapheus	4 ob.
10	metronomoi	4 ob.	10	boōnai	2 ob.
35	sitophulakes	4 ob.	1	grammateus epi ta psēphismata	4 ob.
10	epimelētai tou emporiou	4 ob.	10	epimelētai tōn neōriōn	4 ob.
11	hoi endeka	4 ob.	10	epimelētai tou Amphiareiou	1 ob.
5	eisagōgeis	2 ob.	10	epistatai Braurōnothen	1 ob.
40	hoi tettarakonta	2 ob.	7	epistatai Eleusinothen	4 ob.
5	hodopoioi	4 ob.	10	epistatai tou argurokopiou	2 ob.
10	logistai	2 ob.	10	epistatai tou Asklēpieiou	1 ob.

10	sunēgoroi tois logistais	2 ob.
1	grammateus kata prutaneian	4 ob.
1	grammateus epi tous nomous	4 ob.
1	grammateus tou dēmou	4 ob.
10	hieropoioi epi ta ekthusmata	2 ob.
10	hieropoioi kat' eniauton	4 ob.
1	arkhōn eis Salamina	1 dr.
1	dēmarkhos eis Peiraieia	4 ob.
1	grammateus tois thesmothetais	4 ob.
1	arkhōn eponumos	4 ob.
10	epimelētai eis Dionysia	1 ob.
4	epimelētai mustēriōn	2 ob.
1	basileus	4 ob.
10	epistatai tou hierou tēs Agathēs Tukhēs	1 ob.
1	hieromnēmōn	1 dr.
10	hieropoioi eis Panathēnaia	1 ob.
10	hieropoioi tais semnais theais	1 ob.
9	nomophulakes	1 ob.
10	praktores	2 ob.
2	tamiai toin theoin	4 ob.
1	tamias eis ta neōria	4 ob.
1	tamias kremastōn	2 ob.
1	tamias triēropoiikōn	2 ob.
1	tamias tēs boulēs	4 ob.
1	tamias tou dēmou	2 ob.
200	20 other boards of religious supervisors	1 ob.

TOTAL NUMBER OF MAGISTRATES   658

TOTAL ANNUAL COST   29 t. 3,025 dr.

managing of the sanctuary's finances must have required a full-time commitment (10–22).[168] Importantly this remuneration suggests that the daily rates of *misthos* for magistrates, as was the case with jury pay from the mid-420s, remained unchanged for about a century until the democracy's overthrow in the late 320s. Consequently the figure that we have calculated for the cost of magistrates in the 330s can be used for the 370s and also for the internal *arkhontes* of the 420s.

In this last decade there were around the same number of Athenians again serving as magistrates in their empire's cities. At the daily pay rate of 1 dr. the cost of these extra 658 positions would have been 40 t. 170 dr. per year. In his *Birds* of 415/4 Aristophanes makes his main character offer an Athenian *episkopos*, immediately upon his arrival, his *misthos* in full if he leaves the character's new city without conducting any business (1022–1026). Since Böckh, scholars have taken this passage as evidence that the cities of the *arkhē* had to pay for the magistrates that Athens imposed on them.[169] This inference is supported by a decree of 428/7, which ordered a subject city to provide Athenian *arkhontes* with provisions (*IG* i³ 62.5–7) and by the fact that the allies of Athens' second league, which was much more benign than the empire of the previous century, still had to pay for Athenian garrisons (RO 51.8–12). In forcing them to remunerate its overseas *arkhontes*, Athens was actually imposing a tax on the *arkhē*'s subjects. Thus, the 40 or so talents that they paid Athenian officials every year was a significant part of the income over and above the *phoros* ("tribute") that Athens of the later fifth century earned from its empire.[170] In the 420s the total wages bill for Athenian magistrates was 69 t. 3,195 dr.

UNDERSECRETARIES

Classical Athenians had to pay for the clerical staff of their magistrates. The term that they used most commonly to describe these public employees was *hupogrammateis*.[171] It emphasized how each of them worked under the supervision of a magistrate and looked after his *logos* or accounts.[172] These "clerks of the magistrates were mostly salaried citizens."[173] In two speeches, Demosthenes ridiculed Aeschines for coming from a poor family.[174] As a young man, Aeschines had apparently worked as such a clerk (e.g., Dem. 18.127, 19.70). In mocking this paid work, Demosthenes assumed that every magistracy had a *hupogrammateus*. In the earlier of the speeches, he said that his opponent had served in this role not to some *arkhai* but to "the *arkhai*" (19.200).[175] He went on to mock Aeschines and his brother for making a living as undersecretaries to *hapasai hai arkhai* ("all of the magistracies" — 249). In the later speech, Demosthenes claimed that his opponent began working for "the minor *arkhai*" as soon as he turned eighteen (18.261). If these "*ta arkhidia*" had undersecretaries, the more important ones must also have had them. Certainly other legal speeches imply this to be the case (e.g., Antiph. 6.49; Lys. 30.29).

Not every Athenian magistrate had an undersecretary. Several *arkhontes* were actually *grammateis* of the assembly, council, and some boards of magistrates. What we know of these secretaries shows how they personally kept records and read out documents (e.g., [Arist.] *Ath. Pol.* 54.3–5). Others had more than one employee: in the later fourth century the eponymous archon, *basileus*, and polemarch had two each, who were called *paredroi* or assistants (56.1), while the *hieromnēmōn* apparently had three.[176] Since military commanders tended to be wealthy, they had more than enough education to keep their accounts themselves.[177] I think the same of those who volunteered to be public prosecutors or to fill solitary treasurerships. Thus, I do not think that undersecretaries were provided to the *sōphronistai, kosmētēs, tamias stratiōtikōn, tamias tois adunatois, eisagōgeis, sunēgoroi tois logistais, grammateus kata prutaneias, grammateus epi tous nomous, grammateus tou dēmou, stratēgoi, taxiarkhoi, hipparkhoi, phularkhoi, hipparkhos eis Lēmnon, tamias tēs Paralou, tamias tēs Ammōnos, amphiktuones eis Dēlon, anagrapheus, antigrapheus, tamias eis ta neōria, tamias kremastōn, tamias triēropoiikōn*, and *tamias tou dēmou*. As there was a *grammateus tois thesmothetais*, this board did not need its own *hupogrammateus*. *IG* ii² 1672 and 1673 show how the *epistatai Eleusinothen* and the *tamiai toin theoin* shared an undersecretary.

By this reckoning, Athenian democracy of the 330s employed sixty-four clerical staff for fifty-eight magistracies. In line with the situation for the *arkhai*, this number as well as the pay rates for undersecretaries presumably remained stable from the later fifth to the later fourth centuries. The average of the surviving figures that we have for their *misthos* is 3 ob. per day.[178] At this rate the annual cost of clerical staff in the 330s and the 370s was 1 t. 5,680 dr.[179] In the 420s we have seen how there was the same number of *arkhai* again serving in the *arkhē* (see "Magistrates," above). This suggests that the cost of undersecretaries in this decade was probably double what it was in the next century.

PUBLIC SLAVES

Fourth-century Athens owned a pool of public slaves.[180] They worked either as *hypēretai* ("assistants") for some magistrates or as *ergatai* ("laborers") under the supervision of others. Hansen estimates that the democracy had "not fewer than a thousand" *dēmosioi* or public slaves and "maybe distinctly more."[181] Yet the scattered evidence we have for them suggests that this estimate is too high. Ten *hypēretai* are attested for the council.[182] Another ten certainly helped to operate the lawcourts ([Arist.] *Ath. Pol.* 63.5; 64.1; 65.1, 4; 69.1).[183] The democracy's two testers of coins were also public slaves (RO 25).[184] The *astunomoi* used *dēmosioi hypēretai* to remove the bodies of those who had perished in the street ([Arist.] *Ath. Pol.* 50.2). As they were split between the city and its port, each group of *astunomoi* probably needed five slaves. The *epistatai* of the public mint supervised workers (RO 25.54–55), who were slaves (Andocides fr. 5 Blass and Fuhr).[185] The Eleven took *hypēretai* with them when they went to make arrests or to seize property (Dem. 24.162, 197). They also employed them to man the jail (Pl. *Phdr.* 117e–118a), to execute the condemned, and to torture slaves whose testimony was required in a lawcourt

(Aeschin. 2.126). The supervisors of the dockyards also had *dē-mosioi* as assistants (e.g., Dem. 47.35–36). The supervisors at the mint, the Eleven, and the supervisors at the dockyards probably required no more than ten public slaves per board.

The only figure that survives for a gang of public slaves serving as laborers comes from the accounts of Eleusis from 329/8.[186] They record the payment of seventeen *dēmosioi* who worked in this sanctuary and one *epistatēs* of them who is himself a *dēmosios* (e.g., *IG* ii² 1672.4–5). This may have been by far Attica's largest sanctuary, but there were a few dozen smaller ones scattered across it.[187] Consequently twice this number of *ergatai* again may have been maintaining other sanctuaries (cf. [Arist.] *Ath. Pol.* 50.1). Finally, Attica's road builders employed *dēmosioi ergatai* to repair the roads (54.1). Each of these 5 magistrates could have supervised a gang that was the same size as the one at Eleusis. The total number of public slaves to which this scattered evidence points is 206.

Public slaves lived independently and could have their own houses (e.g., Aeschin. 1.54, 58, 62).[188] So that they could cover their living expenses, Athens of the fourth century gave them *misthos*. The Eleusinian accounts give us the only surviving pay rates.[189] In 329/8 this sanctuary's supervisors and treasurers paid slave laborers and their *epistatēs* 3 ob. per day (*IG* ii² 1672.4–5, 42–43, 117–118, 141–142, 233–234). In addition, they clothed these *dēmosioi*, purchasing for them leather sandals, leather aprons, and other clothes (102–105, 190, 230). Over and above this remuneration the *epistatēs* was paid a *misthos* of 10 dr. per prytany or about 1⅔ ob. per day (5–6, 43, 118, 142–143). There were some public slaves who owned their own houses, had expensive hobbies, and were generally well off (e.g., Aeschin. 1.54). They, clearly, were paid a lot more than the slave laborers at Eleusis. Thus, we can safely estimate that each *dēmosios* cost the Athenians no less than 4 ob. per day. At this rate the wages bill for 206 of them was 8 t. 2,127 dr. per year.

Classical Athens bought rather than bred its public slaves (Aeschin. 2.172–173; Andoc. 3.4–5; RO 25.39–40). To maintain its pool of them, it had to replace those who had died. The yearly rate at which it bought slaves had more or less to match this pool's death rate. As the evidence that is required for ancient Greece's demography is so scarce, the death rate can be calculated only on the basis of a model life table and the assumption of a stable population.[190] The most used tables of this kind were formulated by Ansley Coale and Paul Demeny in the 1960s.[191] Hansen has pioneered their use in the study of the population sizes of Greek *poleis*.[192] Of the Coale-Demeny tables he chooses the model west life table with Mortality Level 4.[193] In it the average life expectancy of males at birth is only 25.3 years.[194] Hansen argues that this table best fits the conditions of antiquity. Given that his choice of Coale-Demeny table has been widely accepted, my calculations are based on it.[195]

Athens needed its new public slaves to start work immediately (e.g., RO 25.39–40). Presumably it wanted them to work for decades. Consequently it is more likely than not that the slaves whom it bought were young adults. This purchasing pattern affected life expectancy significantly. Hansen's Coale-Demeny table is for a high-mortality population in which many deaths occur in the early years of life. This means that those who survive childhood live for a lot longer. Table 3.2 summarizes the makeup of Athenian public slaves.[196] It shows how, following the Coale-Demeny table, the average life expectancy at the age of 20–24 years is 30.6 years, which would suggest that a *dēmosios* lived on average to 50.6 years. This table also summarizes the age distribution of public slaves and their death rates at different ages. Both are calculated on the assumption of a stable number of public slaves who were purchased as young adults. Demographers often calculate the so-called crude death rate by multiplying each age group's proportion of the population by its death rate and adding the results of these multiplications. When we do so, the annual death rate for this pool is 3.3 percent. Thus, every year Athens bought the equivalent of this percentage of its public slaves. When they numbered 206, this equated to 7 new slaves per year.

We have good evidence for the cost of slaves in classical Athens.[197] In legal speeches, the most common price mentioned was 200 dr. (e.g., Dem. 27.9, 18; 41.8; cf. Xen. *Vect.* 4.23), but there were skilled slaves who sold for up to three times more (Dem.

TABLE 3.2 LIFE TABLE OF PUBLIC SLAVES

Age Range in Years	Average Life Expectancy in Years	Percentage of the Population in Age Interval	Age-Specific Annual Death Rate
20–24	30.6	15.8	1.5
25–29	27.7	14.6	1.7
30–34	24.9	13.3	1.9
35–39	22.2	12.0	2.3
40–44	19.5	10.6	2.7
45–49	17.0	9.2	3.2
50–54	14.5	7.7	4.0
55–59	12.2	6.1	4.9
60–64	10.0	4.6	6.8
65–69	8.1	3.1	9.1
70–74	6.3	1.8	12.6
75–79	4.9	0.9	18.1
80+	3.8	0.4	26.3

27.9). This parallels the records of a public auction from 415/4. Athens held it to sell the private property of citizens who had been condemned for parodying the Eleusinian Mysteries in private and mutilating the Herms (Thuc. 6.53, 60). Of the twenty-five slaves whose sale prices survive the average was 174 dr. (*IG* i³ 421.34–49, 422.70–80, 427.4–11).[198] Again, however, a goldsmith sold for 360 dr. and a waiter for 215 dr. (422.71–73, 77–78). All of this suggests that a new public slave would have easily cost 200 dr. on average. Seven of them would have added up to 1,400 dr. Thus, the total amount that *dēmosioi* cost Athens of the 370s and the 330s was 8 t. 3,527 dr. per year.

Athens spent more than twice as much on public slaves in the 420s. At some point in the mid-fifth century it purchased Scythian archers (Aeschin. 2.172–173; Andoc. 3.4–5).[199] Classical writers agree that this corps of *dēmosioi* numbered three hundred.[200] The *Suda* (s.v. *toxotai*) and the scholion on Ar. *Ach.* 54 give their number as one thousand. The classical Athenians did not need so many to carry out the limited duties that they gave these public slaves.[201] This higher figure was probably due to confusion on the part of these two postclassical sources between this force and the army's archers.[202] Thus, the lower number looks more reliable.[203]

The main duty of the Scythian archers was helping the council's *prutaneis* in the assembly "where they seem to have acted a bit like night club bouncers."[204] Consequently they moved citizens loitering in the *agora* towards the hill of the Pnyx when the assembly was about to open (see "Assemblygoers," above). When the executive committee ordered them, they threw out unruly assemblygoers (e.g., Ar. *Ach.* 54, *Eccl.* 143, 258–259; Pl. *Prt.* 319c). They did the same when the *boulē* met (Ar. *Eq.* 665). "Thus the city paradoxically entrusted to real barbarians an active part in the operation of its democracy."[205] At other times, executive-committee members asked the *toxotai* accompanying them to make arrests or to stop riots (e.g., Ar. *Lys.* 387–475; *Thesm.* 929–946). A decree of the 440s or the 430s had Scythian archers man a guardhouse on the Acropolis (*IG* i³ 45.1–5, 14–17).[206] At 4 ob. per day, the yearly cost of remunerating this corps was 12 t. 2,000 dr. To keep them at full strength, Athens had to purchase ten Scythian archers per year. At 200 dr. per slave, this was an additional expense of 2,000 dr. In total, Athens of the 420s spent 12 t. 4,000 dr. per year on this corps.[207]

The last mention of the Scythian archers occurs in a comedy of the late 390s (Ar. *Eccl.* 143, 258–259). Certainly by the midfourth century a group of citizens had taken over the duties that these *toxotai* had once had in the assembly (Aeschin. 1.26, 33–34, 3.4; [Dem.] 25.90).[208] Most scholars believe that this corps was no more by the early 370s.[209] In my costing of *dēmosioi* I follow this majority view. So in the 420s how much in total did Athens spend on public slaves? I cannot see how public slaves, excluding, for the moment, the Scythian archers, could have been fewer than they would be in the next century. Thus, a cautious answer to this question would be the sum of the yearly cost of this corps and that of *dēmosioi* in the 370s and the 330s. Thus, Athens of the 420s spent on public slaves not less than 21 t. 1,527 dr. per year.

GOLD CROWNS

The democracy's last fixed operating cost was gold crowns.[210] "The epigraphical evidence for the conferring of gold crowns is very fitful until almost the middle of the fourth century."[211] In the previous century it is limited to the gold crown that was given to Thrasybulus of Calydon as a reward for assassinating one of the Four Hundred's leaders (*IG* i³ 102.1–14).[212] The Athenians started giving them to magistrates in the 330s.[213] The first gold crown for a politician dates to 343/2 (*IG* ii² 223.A4–13). Some of them were worth 500 dr. each (e.g., 223.A6–8, B7–9; 410.21–22, 34–35; 415.25–27), but the most common value of such a crown was 1,000 dr.[214] The *dēmos* viewed the awarding of them as an incentive (e.g., ii² 223.A13–15; 338.21–24). They did so to encourage more citizens to be magistrates or politicians and to serve them as generously as possible.[215] Stephen Lambert explains that such honors "essentially" were "levers designed to make officials behave well."[216] In the 330s most crowns for *arkhontes* went to wealthy priests, who were now generally spending more out of their own money on the festivals that they helped to run.[217]

For Hansen this incentive "must have been a costly undertaking."[218] He argues that every year the best magistrates and the best politician were awarded gold crowns. In support of such yearly contests he cites *IG* ii² 223 and 415.[219] In the 330s Hansen estimates that such honors cost between 10 and 20 t. per year.[220] At 1,000 dr. per crown, this works out to be 60 to 120 gold crowns.

Hansen's estimate is much too high. The inscriptions he cites do not attest such regular yearly competitions. The first records only a decree that honors a politician who had put in the best performance in the previous year (*IG* ii² 223.A4–5). The second shows only how the awarding of magistrates was governed by a *nomos* or law (415.28–30). Against what Hansen argues, the *dēmos* could actually award as many gold crowns as they liked (e.g., Aeschin. 3.9–10). In spite of this freedom, the surviving inscriptions suggest that they voted no more than once a year on average to confer gold crowns.[221] Admittedly some of these honorary decrees conferred crowns on more than one magistrate (e.g. *IG* ii² 330.15, 41–42, 56–57, 59–62), but the highest combined worth of gold crowns that were awarded on one occasion was only 1 t. 1,000 dr. (410).[222] This figure thus serves as the maximum yearly cost of gold crowns for officials. On top of it we must add the gold crowns that the *dēmos* gave politicians. What evidence we have for them points to no more than one or two more crowns per year (Aeschin. 3.178, 187; Dem. 18.114; *IG* ii² 223.A4–5). The Athenians also conferred gold crowns on foreign benefactors, who normally gave them back as dedications to Athena (Aeschin. 3.46; RO 64.33–38).[223] On average they awarded less than one gold crown to a foreigner each year.[224] All of this suggests that the annual cost of gold crowns for magistrates, politicians, and foreign benefactors was less than 2 t. in the 330s.[225] The first gold crowns for foreigners after the one for Thrasybulus in 410/9 date to 369/8 (*IG* ii² 103.26–30). Consequently gold crowns were not among the democracy's fixed operating costs in the 370s and the 420s.

SETTLING THE BÖCKH-JONES DEBATE

The classical Athenians manifestly spent a lot of public money on subsidizing the poor's participation in politics. Table 3.3 shows how in the 420s this political pay and the democracy's other recurring costs added up to 157 t. per year.[226] These 4.1 tons of silver were 50 percent more than what they spent on worshiping the state's gods.[227] Yet it is by no means certain that they relied on imperial tribute to pay for these running costs. In 432/1, when the Peloponnesian War was about to start, Athens' yearly income was 1,000 t.[228] Six hundred t. of this came from the *arkhē* and 400 t. from internal sources. The *dēmos* apparently reserved the imperial income for military spending and the internal income for nonmilitary spending (Thuc. 2.13.3–6).[229] In the 420s there is no reason to believe that this internal income ever declined.[230] In classical Athens the two major areas of nonmilitary spending were the staging of festivals and the running of the democracy. From 430 to 350 a significant proportion of the 100 t. per year that was spent

TABLE 3.3. THE ANNUAL COST OF THE DEMOCRACY

Fixed Operating Costs	420s	370s	330s
Jurors	53 t. 2,800 dr.	26 t. 4,400 dr.	26 t. 4,400 dr.
Councilors	9 t. 4,625 dr.	11 t. 3,600 dr.	14 t. 3,000 dr.
Assemblygoers	0	20 t.	45 t.
Magistrates	69 t. 3,195 dr.	29 t. 3,025 dr.	29 t. 3,025 dr.
Undersecretaries	2 t. 5,360 dr.	1 t. 5,680 dr.	1 t. 5,680 dr.
Public Slaves	21 t. 1,527 dr.	8 t. 3,527 dr.	8 t. 3,527 dr.
Gold Crowns	0	0	2 t.
TOTAL	156 t. 5,507 dr.	98 t. 2,232 dr.	128 t. 1,632 dr.

on festivals came out of the pockets of wealthy liturgists.[231] Thus, the *dēmos* of the 420s clearly had most of this 400 t. left over to pay for the democracy's fixed operating costs.

In the 420s yearly military spending ended up far exceeding the annual income of 600 t. from the empire.[232] Importantly the Athenians did not fund this shortfall by cutting what they spent on festivals or politics. Instead they used up their cash reserves, taxed the wealthy more heavily, and trebled the *phoros* that the empire's cities paid. Their first attempt to pay for military spending by reducing nonmilitary spending was made only much later in the Peloponnesian War (Thuc. 8.1.3, 8.4). Fifth-century Athenians clearly did not rely on imperial income to pay for its democracy.

Admittedly in the 420s the Athenians did use 40 t. of their imperial income to pay the 700-odd magistrates who helped to run the empire. But this was a choice on their part rather than a necessity; they could have easily covered this wages bill with internal income. Apparently they saw it primarily as a cost of the *arkhē* and so thought it more appropriate for their imperial subjects to pay for it. Table 3.3 tallies too the democracy's annual costs in the 370s and the 330s. These totals support this finding about fifth-century Athens's ability to pay for its democracy without tribute.

The *arkhē*'s loss reduced by half the numbers of magistrates and lawsuits. Consequently the fourth-century democracy always cost less than what it had in the age of Pericles.[233] Yet it still added up to a significant public expense. The 98 t. that the Athens of the 370s spent on it every year matched what was spent on its program of festivals. In the 330s, when the *misthos* for assemblygoers was considerably higher, it spent even more on politics. Without tribute, fourth-century Athenians could cover the democracy's fixed operating costs only out of income that they had raised at home.[234] If they were able to do so, their fifth-century forebears could no doubt have done the same. In this public-spending debate we must thus follow A. H. M. Jones rather than Böckh.

FOUR

THE COST OF WAR

In classical Athens military spending varied greatly from 430 to 350. In the Peloponnesian War's course the Athenians lost no less than 50 percent of their population. Their final defeat in 405/4 brought to an end their income-bearing *arkhē* ("empire"). After this war the *dēmos* ("people") were simply not capable of waging wars on the same scale. This makes it necessary to calculate military spending before and after 405/4. In the 420s the *dēmos* used imperial income for wars and internal income for festivals and politics. For both income types, reliable totals survive. The same applies to the loans that Athens took out and the emergency taxes that it levied to pay for their armed forces. In Chapters 2 and 3 I estimated nonmilitary spending. Consequently it is also possible to calculate how much internal income was left over and so available for military purposes. By adding these figures, this chapter establishes what Athens spent on warfare in the 420s. It uses the annual average of this public spending as the benchmark for costing roughly the rest of the Peloponnesian War.

For the fifty years after this war, no public-spending figures survive. Thus, the only costing method that is available is the isolating of individual costs and the estimating of each on the basis of evidence. This chapter groups these costs of the armed forces into the basic cost classes of modern economics: capital costs, fixed operating costs, and variable operating costs. There is enough evidence to estimate these first two cost classes from the 370s to the 350s. With variable operating costs, this is possible only for the

370s. This chapter thus estimates the full cost of the armed forces in this last decade. It considers too whether military spending remained roughly the same into the 360s.

PUBLIC SPENDING ON THE
ARMED FORCES IN THE 420S

In 432/1, on the eve of the Peloponnesian War, Pericles reassured the assembled Athenians that they had the resources that were needed to win (Thuc. 2.13). As their military strength lay in the money from their subjects, Pericles argued, they should be heartened by the 600 t. they received largely but not exclusively as *phoros* ("tribute") every year (2.13.3; Plut. *Arist.* 24.3). This imperial income also included booty, shipping tolls, the rents of sacred lands overseas, the pay of imperial magistrates, and the indemnities that Athens had imposed on Greek states that it had forcefully prevented from seceding from the *arkhē* (e.g., Thuc. 1.117.3; *IG* i³ 61.39–42, 369.42–43, 370.18–19, 371.16–27).[1] Because the tribute of 433/2, the closest year for which firm evidence exists, was 388 t. (*IG* i³ 279), this nontribute stream of imperial income was probably 212 t. in 432/1, resulting in the total of 600 t.[2] The bulk of this imperial income was managed by the Athenian *hellēnotamiai* ("treasurers of Greece"), who dispersed funds to generals on campaign and paid directly for other military costs.[3]

Pericles carefully distinguished this 600 t. from "the other income" (Thuc. 2.13.3), which was raised internally from, among other sources, the silver mines, taxes, lawcourt fees, rents on sacred land, and public auctions of confiscated goods and properties (e.g., Ar. *Vesp.* 656–660; *IG* i³ 421–430).[4] Xenophon reckoned that the total amount that Athens raised at home and abroad was 1,000 t. at the start of the Peloponnesian War (*An.* 7.1.27), leaving the internal income at some 400 t. per year.[5] In the 420s Athens spent only about half of this sum on running its democracy and its program of festivals.[6] Therefore, it seems safe to assume that 100 t. of this internal income could—if necessary—have been used to pay for the armed forces.[7]

The astronomical cost of the Archidamian War compelled the Athenians relatively quickly to raise their general level of taxation (e.g., Thuc. 2.70.2, 3.17.3).[8] In 428/7 the Athenian people imposed an *eisphora* or emergency tax for war on the property of the wealthy, which raised the unprecedented sum of 200 t. (Thuc. 3.19.1).[9] This tax may have haunted political debates into the late 420s (e.g., Ar. *Vesp.* 923–926). It was, however, probably abandoned for the time being when, in 425/4, Athens massively increased the *phoros* that their subjects were forced to pay to 1,200 t.[10] Indeed a goal of this increase may have been to render the taxing of the wealthy unnecessary. From the surviving list of the new payments that Athens demanded of individual states, the grand total of this tribute reassessment appears to have been slightly over 1,460 t. (*IG* i[3] 71.61–181).[11] Clearly the actual total of *phoros* that the Athenians collected must have been lower, because some city-states on this list had never been or were no longer part of the *arkhē*, while others were in open revolt against Athens.

Yet this new total of tribute was most probably not significantly lower, for Plutarch wrote that *phoros* rose to 1,300 t. after the death of Pericles in 429/8 (*Arist.* 24.3); Andocides said that it reached 1,200 t. after the Peace of Nicias of 422/1 (3.8–9); and Aristophanes claimed, in *Wasps* of 423/2, that the total public income of Athens was nearly 2,000 t. per year (656–660).[12] It is likely that internal income and the nontribute income from the *arkhē* remained more or less unchanged during the Archidamian War.[13] Consequently the figure of Aristophanes translates into tribute of up to 1,388 t. This literary evidence suggests that 1,200 t. would be a safe estimate of *phoros* from 425/4 onwards.

As the Peloponnesian League prepared to invade Attica, Pericles also told the assembly that there was stored on the Acropolis several thousand talents of coined silver and other bullion that they could spend on defending their *polis* ("city-state") as long as they paid back no less in due course (Thuc. 2.13.3–6). These cash reserves lay in the treasuries of Athena and the other gods, for, in 434/3, the Athenians had liquidated the accumulated funds of the imperial treasury, ordering the *hellēnotamiai* to transfer 3,000 t. to Athena, repay all loans to the other gods, and spend whatever remained on the naval dockyards and fortifications (*IG* i³ 52.A, B).[14]

Amazingly a record of how this sacred money was dispersed survives in the form of the so-called *logistai* accounts (figure 4.1), which ostensibly document the debts to Athena and other gods between the Great Panathenaea of 426/5 and its next celebration in 422/1 (*IG* i³ 369.1–2).[15] For these four years the *logistai* ("public auditors") detailed 808 t. of loans and the interest that was owed on each of them at the end of this period (2–97). As the amounts of these twenty loans and the years in which they were made were recorded, the total level of borrowing for each year can easily be calculated. Presumably to record the monies owing as fully as possible, these public auditors also recorded the total amount of loans that each of the sacred treasuries had issued between 433/2 and 427/6 and the interest that had accrued on these loans in the last quadrennium (98–111). Finally, they spelled out the totals of the loans from, and the interest owing to, Athena Polias, Athena Nike, and the other gods from 433/2 to 423/2 (112–120). The grand total of the sacred loans of these eleven years was 5,600 t. (122–123). Although these accounts detail neither individual loans nor annual totals for the years from 433/2 to 427/6, the interest figures that they give for this period put beyond doubt that the vast bulk of the loans in these seven years were issued in the first four years.[16] On the basis of these interest figures and other evidence for sacred loans (e.g., *IG* i³ 364), the editors of the Athenian tribute lists confidently estimated the totals of loans in this seven-year period.[17] As their estimates have long been accepted, they will be integrated into my calculations.[18]

The *logistai* accounts are the key piece of evidence for calculating public spending on the armed forces from 433/2 to 423/2. Although they never indicate the purpose of the sacred loans, there are four reasons why they were probably used exclusively to pay for the Archidamian War.[19] Firstly, putting these interest-bearing loans to a military end is consistent with the advice of Pericles that the *dēmos* could spend their cash reserves on the impending war as long as they paid back no less (Thuc. 2.13.5–6). Since they clearly perceived these reserves as a military asset and acted on

Fragment of a stele of the so-called logistai *accounts on which the
public auditors recorded the loans for the Peloponnesian War that the
Athenians received from their sacred treasuries between 426/5 and 423/2.
Fragment B of the inscription, IG i³ 369, 422/1 BC. Exhibited at the
Epigraphical Museum, Athens, Inv. No. 6741. Photograph courtesy
of the photographic archive of the Epigraphical Museum.*

the advice of Pericles to use this money for the war, it seems likely that they also treated their disbursements as loans as he had implied.[20] Secondly, these accounts may not have consistently indicated the officials who received the twenty loans of 426/5 to 423/2, but, when they did, the recipients were either generals on campaign or the treasurers of Greece (*IG* i³ 369.2–3, 18, 20–21, 26–27, 56), who, as we have seen, had a central role in the financing of campaigns (see above).

The third reason is that the proportion of the annual public income that Athens could direct to the armed forces was manifestly insufficient for covering the cost of this first phase of the Peloponnesian War. For example, the two-year siege of Potidaea from 432/1 cost the public purse 2,000 t. (Thuc. 2.70.2), while the other naval expeditions of these two years consumed around 840 t.[21] As these undertakings alone cost considerably more than the 700 t. of the annual public income that Athens could spend on military affairs, it obviously had to draw heavily on other funds, which, before the *eisphora* of 428/7, were available only in the sacred treasuries on the Acropolis. Finally, in the absence of a major building program during the Archidamian War, the heavy financial demands of warmaking are the only possible explanation for why Athens of the 420s borrowed a massive 5,600 t.[22] Since "the obvious and natural view of Athenian war finance" is that the Athenians exhausted their annual income before borrowing from their gods, the *logistai* accounts do more than evidence another source of military funding.[23] They also confirm that Athens used up all of its available public income for military affairs between 433/2 and 423/2. This means that public spending on the armed forces in the 420s was simply the sum of the income that Athens could spend on military affairs and these attested loans.

Table 4.1 aggregates the various surviving figures for public spending on the armed forces over these eleven years. The grand total for expenditure is 16,334 t., which translates into an unexpectedly high average of 1,485 t. per year.[24] This last figure is supported by the tribute-reassessment decree of 425/4. The overriding purpose of this reassessment was to ensure that the *dēmos* had sufficient money for the ongoing war (*IG* i³ 71.16–17, 46–50).[25]

TABLE 4.1. PUBLIC SPENDING ON THE
ARMED FORCES IN THE 420S

Archon Year	Tribute	Other Imperial Income	Internal Surplus	War Tax	War Loans	TOTAL
433/2	388 t.	212 t.	100 t.	0	76 t.	776 t.
432/1	388 t.	212 t.	100 t.	0	1,145 t.	1,845 t.
431/0	388 t.	212 t.	100 t.	0	1,370 t.	2,070 t.
430/29	388 t.	212 t.	100 t.	0	1,300 t.	2,000 t.
429/8	388 t.	212 t.	100 t.	0	600 t.	1,300 t.
428/7	388 t.	212 t.	100 t.	200 t.	200 t.	1,100 t.
427/6	388 t.	212 t.	100 t.	200 t.	100 t.	1,000 t.
426/5	388 t.	212 t.	100 t.	200 t.	261 t.	1,161 t.
425/4	1,200 t.	212 t.	100 t.	0	130 t.	1,642 t.
424/3	1,200 t.	212 t.	100 t.	0	163 t.	1,675 t.
423/2	1,200 t.	212 t.	100 t.	0	253 t.	1,765 t.
ANNUAL AVERAGE						1,485 t.

Consequently there must have been a reasonably close relationship between the new target for tribute and the anticipated military spending. In view of the general unpredictability of war, the latter would have been based no less on the actual military spending of the recent past than on apparent short-term requirements. This suggests that the closeness of the 1,460 t. or so for assessed tribute and my average of 1,485 t. per year for public spending on the armed forces provide some corroboration of this chapter's calculations.

This public spending was supplemented by the considerable amounts of their own money that wealthy Athenians spent on their trierarchies. This liturgy required a citizen to command a trireme for up to a year. During his trierarchy a trierarch also had to cover its running costs over and above the *misthos* or pay that the state provided his sailors. The average attested cost of a trierarchy was 4,436 dr.[26] Athens had between 100 and 250 triremes at sea between 433/2 and 423/2 (Thuc. 3.17.1–2). The private spending on these military liturgies would thus have ranged from 74 t. to 185 t. per year.[27] These truly enormous costs of naval warfare fully explain why Pericles emphasized the centrality of money in his prewar speeches and why the Athenian *dēmos* of the later fifth and fourth centuries believed that the *dunamis* ("military power") and the security of their state depended on ships, walls, and especially money.[28]

MILITARY SPENDING IN THE REST
OF THE PELOPONNESIAN WAR

The average level of military spending varied considerably between the subsequent phases of the Peloponnesian War from 422/1 to 405/4. The Peace of Nicias of 422/1 heralded five years of markedly reduced military outlays, which allowed Athens to build up once again several thousand talents of cash reserves (Aeschin. 2.175; Andoc. 3.8–9; Thuc. 6.26.2).[29] Yet military spending in this phase was still apparently around 30 percent of the level of the 420s. Between 433/2 and 413/2, regardless of whether the city was at war, the cavalry corps, the squadron of guard ships, and the maintenance of the fleet and other military assets most probably consumed around 300 t. every year (see "The Full Cost of the Armed Forces in the 370s," below). In addition, this peace did not check the established military hyperactivity of the *dēmos*: they reduced Melos and Scione by siege in 421/0 and 416/5 respectively (Thuc. 5.32.1, 5.84–114, 5.116.2–4), and they campaigned around the Peloponnese and Thrace in 418/7 (5.61–62, 5.64–75; *IG* i³ 370.1–23) and against Macedon in the following two years (Thuc. 5.83.4, 6.7.3).

With the sailing of the Sicilian Expedition in 416/5, combined military spending bounced back to its level before the peace, for, while Sicily was not the only theater of operations during the three years of this campaign, by the time the expedition was utterly destroyed, it had cost in excess of 4,000 t.[30] The pay for the varied crews of the 100 Athenian triremes that sailed to Sicily in 416/5 would have been 3,600 t. alone (Thuc. 6.43). The expedition also included large numbers of mercenary soldiers and allies and received significant reinforcements (6.93.4, 7.20.2).

The loss of so many lives and resources in Sicily greatly distressed the Athenians, leaving them without enough ships in their naval dockyards and forcing them to cut the daily pay of sailors from 1 dr. to 3 ob. (Thuc. 8.1.2, 8.45.2).[31] In little more than a year, however, they had tapped their emergency reserve of 1,000 t. to build and to man triremes and had a force of 100 or so ships at Samos (2.24.1–2, 8.15.1–2, 8.30.2). They had this number of ships at sea or based away from Athens for the rest of the so-called Ionian War, with numbers swelling to 150 ships at Arginusae in 407/6 and 180 ships at Aegospotami two years later (Xen. *Hell.* 1.6.24–25, 2.1.20). This naval commitment—along with the terrestrial defense of Attica from Spartan and Theban raids (*Hell. Oxy.* 12.4; Thuc. 7.27.5)—would have kept military spending at about 60 percent of the average level that it had had in the 420s. At 3,000 dr. each per month, the cost of these 100 ships yearround would have been 600 t. The trierarchies required for these ships would have cost 74 t. At this time the main burden of defending Attica fell to the Athenian cavalry.[32] Its regular members, after Sicily, were paid 1 dr. per day, and *hippotoxatai* ("mounted archers") were paid 2 dr. (Lys. fr. VI.75–79 Gernet and Bizos).[33] Their total pay comes to 85 t. per year if we assume a thousand horsemen and two hundred mounted archers (Thuc. 2.13.8).[34] To this combined total of 759 t. per year would have been added the wages of the other land-based troops defending Athens and its countryside, the cost of shipbuilding, and the costs of the warships over and above the 100 that Athens constantly had away.

THE FULL COST OF THE
ARMED FORCES IN THE 370S

The traditional view of fourth-century Athens was that the population losses of the Peloponnesian War and the loss of the incomebearing *arkhē* caused a wholesale decline in its warmaking.[35] It was long argued that the *dēmos* of postwar Athens initiated fewer wars and were reluctant to serve personally when they did so. Consequently mercenaries had to be employed in increasingly large numbers and soon formed the core of the Athenian armed forces. Ancient historians argued that the massive reduction in public income often prevented fourth-century Athens from launching essential fleets and forced those of its generals who did get to sea to loot foreign lands or to join local wars without the authorization of the *dēmos* so that they could pay for their mercenaries.

In making this interpretation, ancient historians took at face value the generalizations that Demosthenes had made about Athenian warmaking in his speeches of the late 350s and the 340s. As part of his efforts to convince the Athenians to wage war against Philip of Macedon, Demosthenes characterized their military behavior as morally questionable and a source of shame.[36] He repeatedly claimed that his contemporaries were falling short of the high standard of fifth-century Athenians, who had constantly performed acts of *aretē* ("courage"), endured *kindunoi* ("dangers") in battle, and won many victories on land and at sea for the sake of just international relations (e.g., Dem. 2.24; 3.23–26; 4.3–4; 9.36, 40; 13.21–35). They were currently ignoring the solemn duty of every citizen to fight for the city (e.g., 2.23–24, 3.3, 4.2–4).[37] By their refusal to serve personally, they behaved as cowards, leaving mercenaries to fight their wars (e.g., 3.35; 4.7–8, 19, 24, 42, 46; 6.36; 8.21; 9.67; 13.4–5).[38] Finally, while they refused to pay the emergency tax on property for war or to provide *misthos* for those actually in the field (e.g., 2.24–25, 8.21–22), they happily spent more public income on, and prepared more carefully for, *polis*-sponsored festivals than they did for any naval expedition (e.g., 1.19–21; 3.11–13, 19, 28, 30–32; 4.35–37). For this young and not yet established politician, the *dēmos* could restore their military reputation only by accepting his strategically questionable proposals for ongoing military adventures in the north.[39]

Over the last quarter of a century the close study of the actual military performance of fourth-century Athens has overturned this bleak interpretation.[40] In addition, it has corroborated the earlier doubts that some ancient historians occasionally raised about the reliability of Demosthenes as a military historian.[41] In particular Leonhardt Burckhardt demonstrates exhaustively that for the armed forces of postwar Athens, "mercenaries were only an important supplement."[42] Admittedly these foreign troops had long served as lightly armed specialists who fought alongside the regular army and were increasingly employed for sieges and year-round campaigns, in which citizens found it difficult to participate because of their social responsibilities.[43] Additionally the acute population losses of the later fifth century made it necessary for wealthy trierarchs, despite the smaller size of fourth-century fleets, to hire noncitizen rowers for their crews.

Yet the backbone of the Athenian armed forces still remained its citizens. Throughout the fourth century, Athenian hoplites and horsemen regularly fought pitched battles in central Greece where their fighting was decisive for the outcome (e.g., Xen. *Hell.* 3.5.18–22, 4.2.16–23, 4.3.15–20).[44] Athenians also kept coming forward for naval service in reasonable numbers (e.g., [Dem.] 50.29; Xen. *Hell.* 5.4.61).[45] Indeed the Athenian *dēmos* waged war more often in the fourth century than previously: they campaigned incessantly from 396 to 386 and then from 378 to 338, with only year-long interruptions.[46] Athens, finally, "still ruled the waves": it launched the fleets that were required to protect its shipping lines to the Black Sea, which were vital for its grain supply (Dem. 18.301–302; Xen. *Hell.* 5.4.61), and was widely recognized as Greece's leading sea power (e.g., Dem. 6.12, 8.45; Diod. Sic. 15.78.4; Xen. *Hell.* 7.1.1).[47]

Athenian democracy's open political debates also helped the fourth-century *dēmos* to find innovative solutions to foreign-policy problems.[48] An early example is their securing of allies to fight the Spartans during the 370s. The Corinthian War had ended badly for the Athenians: the Persians and the Spartans had joined forces to capture their grain ships and hence had forced them to accept the King's Peace of 387/6 (Xen. *Hell.* 5.1.31). This peace recognized the Greek city-states of Asia as Persian subjects; insisted on the autonomy of the other Greeks, which checked the ongoing efforts of the Athenians to reestablish their *arkhē* (e.g., Andoc. 3.15, 36; Xen. *Hell.* 3.5.10); and promised massive military retaliation against any state that broke the peace.[49] The Spartans used this autonomy clause to continue their aggressive interventions in the affairs of other *poleis* (e.g., Xen. *Hell.* 5.2.1–10, 20–31). These developments made it necessary for the Athenians to address their military vulnerability as a matter of urgency and to do so within the constraints of the King's Peace.

The Athenian *dēmos* thus made with maritime states bilateral alliances that explicitly acknowledged this peace (e.g., *IG* ii² 34–35, 41) and, after a failed attempt on the part of the Spartan commander Sphodrias to capture the Piraeus in 378/7, invited peoples who were not Persian subjects to become members of the so-called Second Athenian League (43). In making this invitation, the Athenians promised not to impose a garrison, imperial magistrates, or *phoros* on those who accepted it; to respect their constitution; and to abstain from purchasing or expropriating their properties (43.15–45). Their renouncing of the policies of their fifth-century empire addressed the fear that many Greeks still had of Athens and signaled to Persia's King that league members would indeed be "free and autonomous" (43.19–20). These promises, which were largely kept, proved effective: membership quickly swelled to around sixty or seventy states (43.79–134; Aeschin. 2.70; Diod. Sic. 15.30.2), whose harbors and military contributions helped the Athenians to restore their naval supremacy by twice forcing Sparta to the negotiating table (e.g., Xen. *Hell.* 6.2.1–2, 6.3.18–19).[50]

An important topic in the political debates of fourth-century Athens was the financing of its foreign policy. The public purse may have been significantly reduced, but combatants still needed to be paid properly (e.g., Ar. *Plut.* 112). For naval expeditions this was a logistical necessity: as the trireme lacked the space for the stowing of provisions, its crew required money to purchase daily rations from local markets or private houses (e.g., [Dem.] 50.22, 53–55).[51] There was also no guarantee that rowers would remain with their ships if they did not receive full pay. The conscription of Athenians for rowing is attested only once before 350, when the grain supply was seriously threatened (50.4–7).[52] Normally individual trierarchs (as their forebears had done in the fifth century) hired their *hupēresia* or corps of petty officers and their rowers directly from among those offering their services in the Piraeus or in ports along the way (e.g., 50.7–8, 12–13, 18–19).[53] Because volunteer rowers faced no effective sanction against desertion and could readily find employers elsewhere, they could (and sometimes did) desert their ships if they were not properly provided for (e.g., 50.11–12, 14–16, 25, 36).[54]

Consequently it comes as no surprise that the Athenians, when they were carefully preparing for all-out war against Sparta in 378/7, reformed their collection of the *eisphora* and in the course of the ensuing hostilities gained the approval of their new league's council to collect regular *suntaxeis* or contributions from its members.[55] Another significant reform in this area was the reorganizing of the recruitment of trierarchs in 358/7.[56] In postwar Athens other sources of money for warmaking included the surplus that the city regularly had from the internally raised income and the gifts of gold that it occasionally received from Persian satraps or the Great King.[57]

In spite of these reforms, fourth-century Athenians often did not have in hand the public funds that were needed to pay fully for the naval expeditions that they sent out.[58] Athenian generals met such shortfalls by raising extra funds on campaign.[59] But they did not do so on their own initiative. The *dēmos* authorized the collection of these funds and on what they could be spent. Upon their return, generals gave the *polis* an inventory of what they had raised in the field and any funds left over. Thus, these monies should be classified as public income.[60] The ultimate guarantors, finally, of the funding of naval operations were the state's trierarchs, for, if public funds could not cover the pay of their crews, they were normally forced to do so out of their own pockets ([Dem.] 50.10; Xen. *Hell.* 6.2.14).[61]

A century ago Frank Egleston Robbins estimated the full cost of the Athenian armed forces in the 370s. His analysis of the numbers of ships and troops of this decade's expeditions remains the most thorough ever attempted and hence will be used in this chapter's estimations.[62] But his estimates of the three basic cost classes of Athenian warmaking incorporated the consensus positions of nineteenth-century scholarship on the cost of a trireme, pay rates, and other basic parameters, which have not stood the test of time. Thus, it is necessary for us to estimate again war's capital costs and fixed operating costs in the 370s and the costs of each campaign on the basis of current thinking.

As a sea power, Athens could not escape the significant capital cost of shipbuilding. Every year its assembly decided how many *kainai* or new ships were required, and its councilors forfeited their customary honors at their term's end if these vessels were not built ([Arist.] *Ath. Pol.* 46.1; Dem. 22.8–11; Xen. *Hell.* 7.1.4). Traditionally, ancient historians assumed that the same number of triremes was commissioned year in and year out.[63] Yet this assumption has limited evidentiary support (Diod. Sic. 11.43.3), ignores the ships that Athens regularly captured from its enemies (e.g., Isoc. 16.21) and sits uneasily with its documented practice of intensive shipbuilding to meet military exigencies (e.g., Andoc. 3.5; Thuc. 8.1.3; *IG* i³ 117; cf. Ar. *Ach.* 1351–1353).[64] Instead Vincent Gabrielsen argues: "It seems better to believe that the number of ships to be built in a year was decided by the assembly with due consideration to recent losses and gains and in accordance with current needs and aims and the availability of resources."[65] The surviving evidence for ship stocks during the 370s supports Gabrielsen's argument.

Xenophon tells us that with the failure of Sparta to condemn Sphodrias for his unprovoked attack against the Piraeus in 379/8, the Athenian *dēmos* decided that the King's Peace was broken and so readied for war by putting gates on their harbors, aiding the Thebans, and building *naus* or warships (*Hell.* 5.4.34–35). As part of their preparations they also began more thoroughly scrutinizing their naval capital, for although Athens of the previous century certainly had *epimelētai tōn neōriōn* or supervisors of the dockyards (*IG* i³ 153.18, 236.5–6), they apparently began setting up annual accounts of their warships and their equipment only in the early 370s (*IG* ii² 1604–1632).[66] The supervisors of 377/6 reported just over 100 triremes in the dockyards. In their fragmentary account there are 35 ships that are described as *palaiai* ("old"), 15 as *kainai*, 3 with no description, and 49 for which a description has been lost or was never made in the first place (1604).[67] If we assume that the same proportion of the last 49 ships were "*kainai*," the total of "new" ships would have been 29.

Admittedly the dockyard supervisors of later decades employed this adjective to describe not only ships that had been built during their terms but others that seemed as good as new. The account of 334/3, for example, described ships that had been built in 337/6 and 336/5 as "*kainai*" and that of 326/5, a ship of 332/1 (*IG* ii² 1623.286–289, 294–297; 1628.82–84). This usage makes it possible that some of the "new" ships of 377/6 may have been commissioned as early as the late 380s. Yet in view of Xenophon's testimony and the relative quietism of Athens immediately after the King's Peace of 387/6, it is more likely that all 29 of these were built in 378/7 and 377/6.[68]

In the following years, naval victories swelled the size of the Athenian fleet. At the battle of Naxos, in 376/5, Chabrias captured 49 enemy ships and more than 20 others in ones or twos afterwards (Dem. 20.77; Diod. Sic. 15.34.6). The other surviving dockyard accounts of the 370s described numerous ships and pieces of equipment as *aikhmalōtos* ("won by the spear") under the command of Chabrias, Timotheus, or Iphicrates.[69] Since none of these post-377/6 accounts called a ship "*kainē*," these captures apparently were numerous enough to obviate the need for further shipbuilding.[70]

Robbins accepted Böckh's costing of 2 t. for the hull of a trireme and its equipment.[71] This old estimate is much too high. A fourth-century trierarch had to pay 5,000 dr. for a hull if he was judged responsible for the loss of his warship (e.g., *IG* ii² 1628.339–368).[72] Although the cost of shipbuilding would have fluctuated along with the market prices of its raw materials, this setting of 5,000 dr. as compensation probably implies that this was normally enough to pay for a hull.[73] From the mid-fourth century the accounts of the dockyard supervisors put the value of a complete set of trireme equipment at 2,169 or 2,299 dr.[74] Together these figures suggest 1 t. 1,234 dr. as the cost of a new trireme. This finds some corroboration in the assumption of ancient writers that such a ship could be built for 1 t. (e.g., [Arist.] *Ath. Pol.* 22.7; Plut. *Them.*

4.2; Polyaen. 1.30.6). Therefore, the 29 ships that Athens is likely to have built in 378/7 and 377/6 can be costed at 34 t. 5,786 dr.

The horses of the cavalry corps were another significant capital cost. By the 370s Athens had long helped its wealthy youths to join the corps by providing each recruit with a *katastasis* ("establishment loan") of up to 1,200 dr. for his warhorse (Eup. fr. 293 Kassel and Austin; Lys. 16.6–7).[75] Since a horseman paid the state back only when he retired from the corps, it is possible that he may have been able to offset some of this private expense by selling his horse. The most reliable evidence we have for the cost of such mounts is the lead tablets of the cavalry headquarters that were discovered in wells of the Ceramicus and the *agora* ("marketplace").[76] They recorded the annually adjusted market value of each member's horse.[77] The prices of the nineteen fourth-century tablets that are legible ranged from 100 to 700 dr. and average 408 dr.[78] A member of the cavalry corps also had a *hippokomos* ("groom"), who cared for his horse and carried his equipment and supplies in the field (Thuc. 7.75.5; Xen. *Eq. Mag.* 4.4, 5.6). A safe estimate of how much a horseman spent on a horse for this slave might be 100 dr., which is the lowest recorded horse price we have from the cavalry archive and literary sources (Ar. *Nub.* 21–23; Isae. 5.43; Lys. 7.10; Xen. *An.* 7.8.6).

Athenian cavalrymen probably retired after ten to fifteen years.[79] By their early thirties, wealthy citizens would have started political careers, picked up new social responsibilities as they became the heads of households, and found the physical toils of training and fighting as horsemen increasingly difficult (Xen. *Eq. Mag.* 1.2, 9). In addition, those whose participation in the corps had depended on a *katastasis* would probably have been unable to buy a second warhorse when their first, after a decade or so, was no longer fit for service. Significantly the average depreciation of a warhorse was 100 dr. per year.[80] This means that a horseman could have used the sale of his mount to offset his establishment loan only if he retired within three or four years. Since it is most unlikely that a phylarch would have let one of his tribal unit resign so far short of a regular service period, horsemen ultimately had to pay for their mount and that of their groom out of their own pockets.

In any one year how much was spent on this capital cost? In the 360s Xenophon believed that the cavalry corps had a steady membership of 1,000 (*Eq. Mag.* 1.2, 9–10, 19; 9.3).[81] With an average length of service of 12.5 years, this translates into eight hundred retirements per decade. Therefore, eighty horsemen on average would have retired and hence repaid their *katastaseis* every year. To maintain the corps' strength, the same number had to join and to buy horses for their *hippokomoi* when they joined. The above-mentioned costs for horses thus points to the private spending of 6 t. 4,640 dr. per year on this capital cost.

War's other capital costs were Attica's fortifications, its naval dockyards, and the equipment of its hoplites and horsemen. A dearth of evidence on their basic parameters entirely rules out the estimating of the costs of them.[82] But some, clearly, were very costly. From the archaic period onwards, city walls were "often huge constructions," which "required a great deal of planning, resources, and care in execution."[83] On the dockyards alone Athens probably spent 34 t. per year in the 340s.[84] Isocrates estimated that the *dēmos* had spent a total of 1,000 t. on them in the fifth century (7.66).[85] This means that the sum of the two capital costs that can be estimated, that is, shipbuilding and horses, serves as a safe minimum figure for this cost class. In 378/7 and 377/6 capital costs were thus at least 24 t. 1,533 dr. per year. From 376/5 to 370/69 they dropped to 6 t. 4,640 dr.

The Athenian cavalry also represented a significant fixed operating cost. Xenophon confirms that the Athenian *polis* spent "nearly 40 t. yearly" to have horsemen whom it could deploy immediately when a war broke out (*Eq. Mag.* 1.19). Because the *katastaseis* that retiring members paid back covered the loans that were made to new recruits, these 40 t. must have been for the *misthos* that every horseman received (1.23). Such a sum provided year-round pay for 1,000 horsemen at the rate of 4 obols per day.[86] What survives of *Against Theozotides* by Lysias corroborates this pay rate and suggests that it dated back to the last years of the pre-

vious century. This speech attacked Theozotides for two proposals that he had put to the Athenian assembly, probably in 403/2.[87]
A surviving fragment shows that the subject of one proposal was
the *misthos* of the cavalry corps (fr. VI.73–79 Gernet and Bizos):
"Concerning war this Theozotides put forward the motion that
the horsemen would receive as pay (*misthophorein*) 4 ob. instead
of 1 dr. and the mounted archers 8 obols instead of 2 dr."[88] Lysias
tells us that this proposal was carried (79–81). On the basis of this
fragment the cavalry's fixed operating cost, before 403/2, would
have been more than 50 percent higher than in Xenophon's day,
and, if pay for the cavalry was halved as it was for the other wings
of the armed forces in 412, it would have been more than three
times higher during the first three phases of the Peloponnesian
War.[89]

Critically, gross pay of 4 ob. would normally not have been sufficient to cover a corps member's day-to-day expenses.[90] For example, Iain Spence calculates how a fourth-century horseman had
to spend between 3 ob. and 1 dr. per day (and considerably more
during shortages) on the fodder for his warhorse and that of his
groom.[91] Consequently his *misthos* never fully defrayed the cost of
his horses. Corps members, finally, did not receive any extra pay
when on campaign; there is simply no evidentiary support for the
old view that horsemen received 1 dr. per day in the field.[92] In his
First Philippic of 352/1 Demosthenes suggested that the horsemen
of the year-round amphibious force that he was proposing should
receive a *sitēresion* of 1 dr. per day (4.28–29). But his whole proposal was rejected by the *dēmos* and Xenophon, writing around
the same time, implied that the daily pay for horsemen had long
remained unchanged (*Vect.* 6.1).[93]

Athens in the 370s also kept at sea or had ready for deployment
a fixed number of triremes. The *Paralus* and the *Salaminia* were
employed for the urgent conveying of messages and generals, and
could, if required, play leading parts in naval battles.[94] For each of
these so-called sacred ships, the people elected annually a *tamias*
or treasurer, who was given 12 t. of public funds ([Arist.] *Ath. Pol.*
46.7; Dem. 21.171, 174). Since the *misthos* for sailors was probably
restored to its pre-412 level at the beginning of the fourth cen-

tury, this amount would have covered exactly the pay of a trireme crew for an entire Attic year.[95] That it was so used seems likely: these ships could have been deployed in the ways in which they were only if a full complement of trained sailors was always at hand. These treasurers apparently doubled up as the trierarchs and hence also bore the regular out-of-pocket expenses of this liturgy (Dem. 21.171, 174; Isae. 5.6; Plut. *Them.* 7.5). With the inclusion of these two trierarchies, the total of this fixed operating cost would have been 25 t. 2,872 dr.

Athens in the fifth century regularly had twenty guard ships at sea ([Arist.] *Ath. Pol.* 24.3; cf. Thuc. 8.74.2–3). Direct evidence may be lacking for it deploying a similar force in the next century, but this too seems likely.[96] Guard ships were manifestly required: in the years before the King's Peace, and again in the 370s, pirates and Spartan ships sailed out from Aegina to attack Attica and its coastal shipping (Xen. *Hell.* 5.1.1–25, 6.2.1). That Athens took action against these threats is clearly implied by what Xenophon writes of the herculean efforts of Iphicrates to man a large fleet in 373/2 (*Hell.* 6.2.14): "He also obtained from the Athenians whatever war-ships were cruising here or there in the neighbourhood of Attica, as well as the *Paralus* and the *Salaminia*, saying if matters in Corcyra turned out successfully, he would send them back many ships."[97] In light of the reduced circumstances of postwar Athens, scholars normally assume it had around half the number of guard ships that it had in the previous century (cf. *Hell.* 2.2.20). Because the coasts of Attica could have been easily attacked any time during the sailing season of eight months, the average length of service of these ships may well have been six months.[98] The combined salary and trierarchic expenses of such a force was 67 t. 2,360 dr.

Smaller fixed operating costs were for the hoplites who manned the forts on Attica's borders and the sons of the war dead whom the state supported until they turned eighteen years old.[99] We may have likely daily pay rates for both groups,[100] but in the absence of evidence for their numbers, once again we cannot estimate these costs. In the mid-330s Athens created a state-subsidized, full-time training program for its future hoplites.[101] We know the number of Athenians who participated in this *ephēbeia* or cadetship each year and the daily *misthos* that they each drew ([Arist.] *Ath. Pol.* 42.3).[102] On the basis of these general parameters, we can cost the *ephēbeia* at "some 25 t."[103] Yet there is no firm evidence for an integrated and publicly funded program of activities for *ephēboi* ("ephebes") before 336/5.[104] I thus do not include *ephēboi* as a fixed operating cost of the Athenian armed forces in the 370s. In this decade the fixed operating costs that can be estimated add up to 132 t. 5,236 dr. Therefore, before Athens sent out a fleet or an army, it spent no less than this total every year on its armed forces.

For the 370s Robbins identified eleven distinct campaigns and determined their chronologies on the basis of the modern calendar year.[105] In estimating war's variable operating costs in this decade, this chapter employs the numbers of troops and ships he worked out for these campaigns and assigns the campaigns to archontic years. Consequently it assigns his Campaign 2 and the first two months of his Campaign 3 to 378/7; the remaining four months of his Campaign 3 and his Campaign 4 to 377/6; his Campaign 5, the first four months of his Campaign 6 and the first four months of his Campaign 7 to 376/5; the remaining four months of his Campaign 6 and the remaining eleven months of his Campaign 7 to 375/4; the first nine months of his Campaign 8 and the first three months of his Campaign 9 to 374/3; the next twelve months of his Campaign 8, the remaining four months of his Campaign 9 and the first three months of his Campaign 10 to 373/2; the remaining twelve months of his Campaign 8 and the remaining twelve months of his Campaign 10 to 372/1; and his Campaign 11 to 370/69.

This chapter splits trierarchic costs equally between archontic years, when a naval venture straddles the two. Since wealthy citizens were obliged to bear this military liturgy for only twelve months at any one time and could claim a two-year exemption from all liturgies after the undertaking of this public service (e.g., [Dem.] 50.39; Isae. 7.38), its calculations include a second set of trierarchs if an expedition went for more than a year.[106] I assume that the cost of a trierarchy was 4,436 dr., the gross pay of a soldier or sailor 1 dr. per day and the total pay of a trireme crew 1 t. per

TABLE 4.2. THE FULL COST OF THE
ARMED FORCES IN THE 370S

Archon Year	Capital Costs	Fixed Operating Costs	Variable Operating Costs	TOTAL
378/7	24 t.	133 t.	72 t.	229 t.
377/6	24 t.	133 t.	112 t.	269 t.
376/5	7 t.	133 t.	787 t.	927 t.
375/4	7 t.	133 t.	858 t.	998 t.
374/3	7 t.	133 t.	229 t.	369 t.
373/2	7 t.	133 t.	500 t.	640 t.
372/1	7 t.	133 t.	787 t.	927 t.
371/0	7 t.	133 t.	0	140 t.
370/69	7 t.	133 t.	60 t.	200 t.
ANNUAL AVERAGE				522 t.

month.[107] Table 4.2 summarizes the results of these calculations and adds up the figures of the three cost classes. The annual high of nearly 1,000 t. and the low of only 140 t. once again bear out the great variability in military spending from year to year. The annual mean of the full cost of the Athenian armed forces from 378/7 to 370/69 was 522 t.

MILITARY SPENDING IN THE 360S

Admittedly the absence of consistently detailed evidence for the campaigns of the 360s reduces the reliability and the granularity of any estimate of military spending in this decade.[108] However, what can be established with some confidence about this decade's scale of campaigns suggests that the overall level of military spending was no less than what it was in the 370s. The battle of Leuctra of 371/0 completely destroyed Sparta as a regional power and gave the Athenians their long-desired opportunity to regain control of the Chalcidice and the Chersonese that they had lost at the end of the Peloponnesian War.[109] For the subsequent campaigns George Cawkwell consolidated the evidence for ship numbers thirty years ago (e.g., Diod. Sic. 15.71.3–4).[110] His conclusion has been widely accepted: "All in all, it would not be surprising if the Athenians had 40 or 50 ships a year out on active service in the 360s."[111]

The generally smaller naval expeditions of the early to mid-fourth century lasted longer on average than those of the Peloponnesian War's first phase: in the 360s alone two expeditions went for more than six months and another three for a year or more.[112] Iphicrates and his forces were at Amphipolis from September 369 to May 365.[113] Timotheus left Athens with 30 ships in July 366, took Samos in May 365, and then moved north for two years of campaigning in the Chalcidice.[114] Ergophilus spent six months defending Sestus in 363/2 (Dem. 2.104).[115] Timomachus campaigned in the region for the full term of his generalship in 362/1 ([Dem.] 50), while Cephisodotus commanded a small fleet in the Hellespont for seven months in 360/59 (Dem. 23.165).[116] In this context a safe assumption for the average length of service for Athenian warships, including guard ships, would be six months.[117] To keep at sea for this time, the 45 ships that Cawkwell proposed would have cost the public purse and wealthy trierarchs 333 t. 1,620 dr. per year.[118]

Although there is no reason to believe that war's fixed operating costs increased in the 360s, capital costs were probably several times higher. At the close of the previous decade, Athens' dockyards would have had no more than 165 warships.[119] By 357/6, the next year for which a naval inventory survives, the total had risen to 283 (*IG* ii² 1611.5–9). As the intervening period saw "no great captures," Athens of the 360s must have built a lot more ships than in the previous decade.[120] Since the average lifespan of a trireme was probably twenty years, half of the original 165 ships would have retired in the course of the 360s.[121] Thus, simply to keep ship numbers steady would have required the *boulē* ("council") to commission 8 ships per year on average. In the thirteen years from 370/69, another 9 new ships per year were needed on average to increase ship numbers to where they were in 357/6. At a construction cost of 1 t. 1,234 dr. per trireme, the average sum that Athens of the 360s spent on shipbuilding was thus 20 t. 2,978 dr. per year. As the total cost of the cavalry's horses probably did not change, this sustained shipbuilding would have increased capital costs to no less than 27 t. 1,618 dr. per year. For the 360s the public and the private spending on the Athenian armed forces that can be estimated adds up to some 401 t.

Yet this total amount does not include the *misthos* of the mercenary and citizen soldiers whom the Athenians of the 360s regularly deployed to bolster the trireme crews of their expeditions. The one surviving set of basic parameters for such deployments suggests that they were a huge variable operating cost: Isocrates tells us that Timotheus employed eight thousand peltasts during his ten-month siege of Samos in 366/5 (15.111–112). Their pay alone would have been 406 t. In conclusion, it is highly likely that the full cost of the Athenian armed forces would have continued at the average level of 500 t. per year into the 360s.

FIVE

CONCLUSION

Public-Spending Priorities

This book refutes Böckh's negative view of what classical Athens spent on festivals. It shows the literary evidence that Böckh cited in defense of his view to be unreliable. The major activities of this *polis* ("city-state") were religious celebrations, democratic politics, and military campaigns. There is no doubt which of them the *dēmos* ("people") saw as their highest priority. In this book I certainly confirm that Athenian *heortai* ("festivals") were generously funded. At 100 t. per year, festivals cost the same as Athenian democracy in the 370s. Even in the 420s, when the government was larger, spending on festivals still equaled two-thirds of what was spent on politics. Clearly Aristophanes was right to argue that the athletic and the musical *agōnes* ("contests") of Athenian festivals depended on wealth (*Plut.* 1161–1163). Of the full cost of these religious celebrations, the City Dionysia and the Great Panathenaea accounted for 35 percent. Demosthenes thus focused with reason on these two *heortai* in his unfavorable remarks about public spending (4.35–37).

Yet this book puts beyond doubt that in classical Athens vastly more was always spent on the armed forces. In times of war this spending easily surpassed the combined costs of festivals and politics. In the 370s the total of public and private spending on *polemos* ("war") was 500 t. per year. At the time this was five times as much as the Athenians were spending on their festivals or democracy. With imperial income and enormous cash reserves, their fifth-century forebears were able to spend a great deal more. In the 420s public spending alone on the armed forces was 1,500 t.

per year. This was fifteen times higher than spending on festivals and ten times higher than public spending on politics. In times of peace the armed forces still cost a great deal. In the 370s their capital costs and fixed operating costs added up to 150 t. per year. This was 50 percent more than spending on either of the state's other major activities. In the 420s Athens paid its cavalry corps treble what it would in the 370s and had double the number of triremes guarding Attica's coasts. Consequently, even before they sent out a military expedition, the Athenians of the later fifth century spent more on their armed forces than they did on festivals *and* politics combined. These cost estimates thus bring the public-spending debate about festivals and wars to an end: the classical Athenians always lavished many times more money on *polemos* than they did on the worship of their gods.

The two literary passages that Böckh presented in support of his negative view are unreliable. The comparison that Demosthenes drew between the disordered *polemos* of his contemporaries and their ordered *heortai* was part of his ill-conceived attempt as a young politician to shame the *dēmos* into fighting Philip the Second (4.35–37).[1] For the classical Athenians, orderliness, which was denoted by *eutaxia*, *eukosmia*, and similar terms, both encouraged citizens to be *sōphrones* ("moderate") and law abiding and underwrote their success in battle (e.g., Aeschin. 1.22–27, 33–34; Dem. 18.216; Xen. *Mem.* 3.1.17).[2] By describing their military activity as "disordered (*atakta*), uncorrected, and indeterminate," Demosthenes was thus criticizing his fellow citizens for their lack of an important civic virtue (Dem. 4.36).

Demosthenes' criticism of the *dēmos*, however, did not end there. Certainly he was not criticizing them for staging festivals. In themselves, *heortai* could not be criticized: they maintained the *kharis* ("sense of gratitude") that the gods had for the state and gave its citizens holidays. Instead he was criticizing his fellow citizens for preparing more carefully for them than for war and for spending more on their two major festivals than on a solitary naval expedition (4.35–37). This preference for the *terpsis* ("delight") of festivals over the *ponoi* ("toils") of war aligned them with the feast-loving but unwarlike Phaeacians of Homer and, worse still, the historical Ionians, whose soft living was thought by the classical Athenians to have made them unwilling to fight in defense of their own freedom (e.g., Hdt. 1.143, 5.68, 6.11–14; Thuc. 1.99).[3] Thus, this comparison of Demosthenes cast into doubt the *aretē* ("courage") of contemporary Athenians.

These and other aspersions that Demosthenes made about Athenian warmaking were manifestly false. In particular, the *dēmos* of fourth-century Athens usually spent several times more on a naval expedition than they did on the City Dionysia and the Great Panathenaea. In 352/1, when Demosthenes delivered his assembly speech, a naval expedition from Athens probably had thirty ships and was away for six months.[4] The 35 t. per annum that the Athenians spent on these two festivals would have kept such a fleet at sea for little more than one month. Indeed, in the course of his speech, Demosthenes actually undercut his own claim about public spending when he costed the small amphibious force that he was proposing at more than 90 t. (4.28). Therefore, his so-called *First Philippic* bears witness to the unexpected license that the Athenian *dēmos* gave their politicians, their tolerance of unwarranted criticism, and the attraction of foreign affairs for ambitious politicians as a topic of debate where they could more easily distinguish themselves.[5]

Less unexpected is the claim of Plutarch that fifth-century Athens spent more on tragic productions than they did on maintaining its empire or fighting the Persian Wars (*De glor. Ath.* 349a). This claim was made in an epideictic oration of the late first century of our era, which Plutarch probably delivered at Athens (345f).[6] This oration's unusual argument was that the generals and the military victories of classical Athens were more deserving of praise than its historians, orators, poets, and visual artists (e.g., 345c, 346f, 347c). This argument may have belittled Plutarch's métier as a writer, but it gave him ample opportunities to display his rich knowledge of Athenian history, literature, and art. Since *On the Glory of Athens* was not a serious analysis of classical Athens, its manifestly wild exaggerations about public spending should not be taken at face value.

This book does more than settle public-spending debates. In

classical Athens the *dēmos* fully controlled public spending. In the assembly they were told the cost of a proposal that was put to them and the proportion of the state's income that it would use up. They had a good general knowledge of what they normally spent on their major public activities. In voting on a proposal, the *dēmos* were thus not just judging its merits, they were also deciding whether they should maintain or change their normal spending pattern. Such votes allowed them to spend more on what they saw as a priority and less on what was less of a priority. Over time the sums that the *dēmos* spent on different public activities consequently reflected the order of the priorities that they had set for their *polis*. The costings of this book leave little doubt as to what this order was. Clearly the *dēmos* judged the worship of their deities equally as important as their own participation in politics. The enormous difference, however, between the combined costs of these two activities and the cost of the armed forces suggests that they saw *polemos* as their topmost public priority. This difference thus casts into doubt the often-expressed view that religion was their most important activity.[7] That war instead was their overriding priority is corroborated by what else we know of its place in classical Athens.

The Athenian *dēmos* were immensely proud of their military history. They viewed military service as a significant contribution to their *polis* and as the surest way to confirm their own *aretē*. For them the battles they fought always enhanced their state's international standing. The regular speeches for the war dead show vividly how the *dēmos* saw themselves as more courageous than the other Greeks; their reasons for fighting battles as always just; and the history of Athens, since the age of the heroes, as an almost unbroken series of military victories.[8] In addition, they saw fighting a battle as an opportunity for individuals and themselves as a collectivity to put their courage beyond doubt (e.g., Dem. 3.23–26, 10.24–25, 10.74, 13.21–35; Lys. 18.24, 30.26).[9] In court, wealthy Athenians characterized their participation in battles as an *agathon* ("public benefaction"), which, along with their liturgies and their paying of war taxes, should make the jurors feel *kharis* towards them (e.g., Lys. 7.41, 12.38, 16.13–18, 18.24–27, 21.5–

FIGURE 5.1.
*Fragment of a relief sculpture of the public list of the war dead from
394/3 showing a horseman attacking two hoplites in the rout at the end
of a battle. Athens, National Archaeological Museum, Inv. No. 2744.
Photograph courtesy of H. R. Goette.*

11, 25.4, 25.12–13, 30.26).[10] By reason of his military service, the
poor citizen too was recognized to be a *khrēstos politēs* ("a good
and useful citizen") or *khrēsimos tēi polēi* ("good and useful to the
state").[11] The *ponoi* that the Athenians bore in battles were repeatedly said to bring benefits: they had secured the security, military
power, alliances, and other international advantages that Athens
enjoyed.[12] This military activity was constantly glorified and legiti-
mized in the state's political debates, religious festivals, and public
art and monuments (figure 5.1).[13]

Athenian democracy simply lacked the sustained critique of

war and violence that is a feature of democracies today.[14] Indeed the *dēmos* took a dim view of any politician who criticized *polemos* as an activity (e.g., Aeschin. 2.74–75; Dem. 19.16) or mentioned their losses on the battlefield (Ar. *Lys.* 37–85, 88–90, *Pax* 647–656).[15] Consequently politicians who wanted to argue against a proposal for a war could do so only on pragmatic grounds (e.g., Thuc. 3.42–49).[16] On separate occasions, for example, Aeschines and Andocides advocated a peace treaty on the grounds that it would allow Athens to build up its cash reserves and armed forces so that it could prosecute wars more successfully in the future (e.g., Aeschin. 2.173–177; Andoc. 3.1–12).[17]

Admittedly comedy and tragedy did provide "safe" opportunities for representing peace's joys or war's costs.[18] Aristophanes, for one, blamed politicians for needlessly starting or prolonging the Peloponnesian War and presented the pleasures that peace brought individuals, while Euripides, because of the faraway settings of *Hecuba* and *Trojan Women*, could focus on the suffering of defeated barbarians and the war crimes of *other* Greeks.[19] Yet both genres also confirmed *aretē* and fighting battles as norms, reinforced the regular characterization of warmaking of classical Athens as just, and besmirched the morality of its major military opponents.[20] When they are thus viewed as a whole, comedy and tragedy did not moderate the manifestly pro-war culture of Athenian democracy.

Polemos was not only held in the highest possible esteem by the classical Athenians. It also dominated their politics and lives. Foreign policy was a major subject of debate in politics and in the lawcourts.[21] War and peace were a compulsory agenda item of the main assembly meeting of each prytany (Ar. *Ach.* 19–27; [Arist.] *Ath. Pol.* 43.4).[22] Consequently politicians also required detailed knowledge of the state's armed forces and those of its main rivals (e.g., Arist. *Rh.* 1359b34–1360a5).[23] The Athenians, moreover, bore the *ponoi* and the *kindunoi* ("dangers") of war much more often than they enjoyed the benefits of peace. In the fourth century they fought constantly from 396 to 386 and from 378 to 338, with only brief periods of respite.[24] In the previous century they waged wars in two out of three years and campaigned on multiple fronts from 431 to 404.[25] Indeed by the 450s the Athenians viewed service on military expeditions as the solemn duty of every citizen.[26] Whether by land or sea, these expeditions involved many thousands of combatants.[27]

In voting for such expeditions, the *dēmos* knowingly accepted that many could be killed in action. For example, in 460 one of the ten Cleisthenic tribes lost 177 men in battles in Greece, Cyprus, Egypt, and Israel/Palestine (*IG* i[3] 1147). Even more extraordinary is the human cost of the Peloponnesian War: in 431 there were probably 60,000 Athenians living in Attica, but, after twenty-five years of this war, only 25,000 remained.[28] Therefore, the cultural militarism of this democracy, its incessant warfare, and the enormous costs of its wars both in lives and in treasure leave no doubt that the Athenian people held their topmost public priority to be war.

NOTES

1. This book was translated remarkably quickly into English (Böckh 1828).

2. Böckh 1828: Volume 1, 360–361 (Book 2 Chapter 21).

3. Böckh 1828: Volume 1, 280 (Book 2 Chapter 12).

4. Burckhardt 1996: 215–224. For its date, see Cawkwell 1962a: 122–127; Milns 2000: 206.

5. *De glor. Ath.* 349a. Translation by Csapo and Slater (1994: 149).

6. E.g., Böckh 1928: Volume 1, 280–302 (Book 2 Chapters 12–13), 332–393 (Book 2 Chapters 19–29); Volume 2, 199–222 (Book 3 Chapters 21–23).

7. Brock and Hodkinson 2000: 4–5; Rhodes 2003: 25–26.

8. Lewis 1997: 4; Sandys 1910: 99.

9. Lewis 1997: 5; Sandys 1910: 98–99.

10. Hedrick 1999.

11. For this attribution, see, for example, Diog. Laert. 5.27.

12. Walters 1891.

13. For its date, see Rhodes 1981: 51–57.

14. E.g., Hignett 1952: 28–30; Rhodes 1981: 61–63.

15. Baldry claims (1971: 33): "The German scholar Böckh estimated direct Athenian state expenditure on all festivals of 25 to 30 talents." As *The Public Economy of Athens* gives no such estimate, this claim appears to be erroneous.

16. E.g., Walton 1977.

17. Winkler and Zeitlin 1990.

18. Parker 1996: 5–7, 92 and 2005: 253–254; P. Wilson 2000: 164–165.

19. Csapo and Slater 1994: 119–121, 141 *pace* Baldry 1971: 32–34.

20. P. Wilson 2000: 95; cf. 2003: 168.

21. P. Wilson 2008: 88.

22. P. Wilson 2008: 119.

23. E.g., Sandys 1897: 109–110 with bibliography.

24. Csapo and Slater 1994: 141.

25. Kallet 1998: 47; P. Wilson 2008: 119. *Contra* Golden 1998: 164–165.

26. E.g., Sourvinou-Inwood 1990: 322. This view goes back to Fustel de Coulanges' *La cité antique* of 1864 (Hansen 2006a: 118). It is closely related to the view that the *polis* developed in the first place out of the communal cooperation that was required to run local cults and to build temples (e.g., de Polignac 1995: 150–154). Rune Frederiksen's exhaustive study of the fortifications of archaic *poleis* strongly challenges this related view (2011: esp. 100–101, 110–111, 119). Frederiksen concludes (119): "Since, however, fortification walls are in fact more commonly attested than temples before the sixth century, that they sometimes occur at sites before temples, and that the defence circuit in fact is found more often than any other type of architectural monument before classical times, it seems valid to suggest that the *polis* developed just as much as a secular as a religious community."

27. E.g., Jameson 1999: 339.

28. Bowden 2005: 159.

29. Bowden 2005: 10, 156.

30. E.g., Cook 1990: 95; Gabrielsen 2007: 256–260 and 2013: 333–335; Pritchard 2005a: 16 and 2010: 6; van Wees 2000: 81. For his part, Böckh wrote of the "unusually large and inevitable expenses" of Athenian military activity and how even "large sums were expended upon naval preparations in time of peace" (1828: Volume 1, 333, 338–339 [Book 2 Chapters 19–20]).

31. Gabrielsen 1994: 115 and 2013: 334; Samons 2000: 209; cf. Baldry 1971: 34. The exceptions are Brun 1983: 144–161; Cook 1990; Robbins 1918; Unz 1985.

32. E.g., Gabrielsen 1994: 114–118; Raaflaub 2007: 109; Samons 2000: 207; van Wees 2000: 107–108; cf. Hansen 1991: 316; Kallet 1998: 46.

33. De Ste. Croix 1981: 290–291.

34. Chapter 3.

35. Hansen 1991: 36–39; Pritchard 1994: 133–135; Rhodes 1981: 318–319.

36. Pritchard 2010: 58.

37. Pritchard 2013: 4, 8–9, 57–58.

38. Rosivach 2001: 127, 133.

39. Rhodes 1981: 338.

40. Sinclair 1988: 120–121.

41. De Ste. Croix 1975 and 1981: 602–603 n. 24; Finley 1978: 310 n. 53 and 1983: 34; Rhodes 1981: 338.

42. Pritchard 2013: 64–65.

43. Pritchard 2013: 57–58, 65–66.

44. *Pace* Ober 1989: 158 and Thomas 2009: 39–41, 42.

45. Böckh 1828: Volume 2, 409 (Book 4 Chapter 22).

46. For his preference, see, for example, Böckh 1828: Volume 2, 412 (Book 4 Chapter 22). For this consequence of the French Revolution, see Keane 2010: 392–396.

47. Wood 1988: 10–16, 19–22 *pace* Lewis 1997: 3.

48. Böckh 1828: Volume 1, 303 (Book 2 Chapter 14).

49. Böckh endorsed completely the criticism of Pericles in Plato's *Gorgias* (515e): by introducing this *misthophoria* he had made the Athenians lazy, cowardly, talkative, and greedy (1828: Volume 1, 290 [Book 2 Chapter 13]).

50. Böckh 1828: Volume 1, 303 (Book 2 Chapter 14).

51. Böckh 1828: Volume 1, 291 (Book 2 Chapter 13).

52. Pritchard 2010: 3–4.

53. E.g., Mahaffy 1892: 16–17.

54. Hansen 1976: 133; A. H. M. Jones 1957: 5, from which the quotation comes; Sinclair 1988: 200.

55. The chapter of A. H. M. Jones 1957 in which he did so was first published as A. H. M. Jones 1952.

56. A. H. M. Jones 1957: 5.

57. A. H. M. Jones 1957: 6.

58. Finley 1973b: 245 n. 52 and 1978: 310 n. 54.

59. Finley 1973a: 49–50.

60. Finley 1973a: 48–49; 1973b: 173; and 1978: 122–123.

61. Finley 1973a: 50.

62. Burke 2005: 8, 10, 13, 25; Hansen 1976: 133; 1987: 48; and 1991: 18–19; Kallet-Marx 1994: 247; Ober 1989: 23–24; Samons 2000: 207; Sinclair 1988: 200–202; cf. Cook 1990: 94 n. 90. De Ste. Croix 1981: 602–603 n. 24 equivocates surprisingly on which side to take.

63. A. H. M. Jones 1957: 5–6.

64. A. H. M. Jones 1957: 6.

65. Chapter 4.

66. A. H. M. Jones 1957: 6.

67. For his part, A. W. Gomme thought it "impossible to say" how much Athens spent on "internal purposes" (1956: Volume 2, 19).

68. Hansen 1976.

69. Hansen 1976: 133.

70. He has gone on to repeat this claim (e.g., Hansen 1987: 48 and 1991: 318–319).

71. Sinclair 1988: 201-202.

72. Hansen 1991: 150, 189, 241, 254-255, 315-316.

73. E.g., Kallet 1998: 46; Möller 2007: 379; Pritchard 2012b: 39 n. 135.

74. See the section entitled "The Period of Eighty Years for Comparing Costs," below.

75. Quotation from Osborne 2007: 14-15. For the flurry of new festivals in the democracy's first fifty years, see Osborne 1993: especially 27-28. For this stability in liturgical numbers and expenditure, see Christ 2006: 163; P. Wilson 2000: 89-93 and 2008: 112.

76. For this loss of population, see Akrigg 2007: 29-33; Hansen 1988: 14-18; Pritchard 2010: 6.

77. Unz 1985: 24-27.

78. Unz 1985: 25 n. 15.

79. Samons 2000: 305-311.

80. Rosivach 1985 (1992).

81. Cook 1990: 80-82; Gabrielsen 2008: 56; Loomis 1998: 39-44, 55-56 with bibliography.

82. Loomis 1998: 36-39; van Wees 2004: 237, 316 n. 27.

83. Chapter 4.

84. Brun 1983: 144-145; Robbins 1918: 361-363.

85. Brun 1983: 162-163; Burckhardt 1995: 124; Heskel 1997: 13-15; cf. Cawkwell 1963: 47.

86. This is in spite of the excellent work that Julia Heskel has done on the chronology of the 360s (1997: especially 159-181).

87. Brun 1983: 154.

88. Burckhardt 1995: 115, 125; Hornblower 2002: 264-265.

89. With Cawkwell 1963: 61-62 n. 85.

90. Cawkwell 1963; Hansen 1991: 98, 263-264; E. M. Harris 2006: 121-139; Rhodes 1981: 513-515 and 2013: 219-220.

91. Csapo 2007: 100-103; Ruschenbusch 1979 with the primary sources. Quotation from Ruschenbusch 1979: 308. Roselli commendably makes the strongest possible case for some form of *theōrika* from the mid-fifth century (2009 and 2011: 87-117), but the weight of the classical-period evidence for such a payment makes it more likely that it was introduced a century later.

92. The Athenian general Chares, for example, probably campaigned in the north with a fleet of thirty ships from 353/2 to 346/5, while Athens sent no less than three expeditions to aid Olynthus during 349/8 (Burckhardt 1995: 114; Cawkwell 1962a: 130, 139 and 1984: 334-335—all with testimonia). Each year Athens probably had on average forty to fifty ships at sea in the 460s (Chapter 4).

93. Cawkwell 1963: 53–54; Hansen 1991: 315–316.

94. Lambert 2012: 185–187; Osborne 2007: 15.

95. Humphreys 2004: 77–129; Lambert 2005; Parker 1996: 242–253; Rhodes 2013: 224.

96. Parker 1996: 124 and 2005: 471–472; Rhodes 2009: 8–9.

97. Aleshire 1994: esp. 14–15; Ostwald 1986: 137–174.

98. Parker 1996: 125.

99. Clinton 2008: 41–42; Rhodes 2009: 2.

100. For these landing taxes, see Parker 1996: 125; Rhodes 2009: 2. For this poll tax, see Jameson 1980; Pritchard 2013: 102; Rhodes 2009: 8.

101. Lewis 1997: 261–262.

102. Rhodes 2009: 9.

103. Clinton 2008: 54; Davies 2004: 504–505; Rhodes 2013: 213, 229; Samons 2000: 135–136, 294.

104. Clinton 2008: 53–54; Rhodes 2009: 4. For the decree's date, see Clinton 2009: 53; Rhodes 2008: 501, 505.

105. Clinton 2008: 54; Linders 1975: 38–57; Rhodes 2013: 213–214.

106. Chapter 4.

107. Gabrielsen 1994: 134–136.

108. Chapter 4.

109. Blamire 2001: 114; Samons 2000: 239.

110. Blamire 2001: 121.

111. Kallet-Marx 1994: 229–230; Rhodes 1972: 88–113.

112. In the Roman Republic the senate had a comparable financial role (Polyb. 6.31.1; Norena 2011: 250).

113. Rhodes 2013: 209.

114. With Rhodes 1981: 553.

115. For the *apodektai*, see Rhodes 2013: 210; Rhodes and Osborne 2003: 82–83.

116. Rhodes 1972: 95.

117. For the *hellēnotamiai* and the imperial treasury, see Rhodes 1972: 102 and 2013: 210, 213–214.

118. Kallet-Marx 1994: 246–247; Rhodes 2013: 209, where they are so described.

119. Rhodes 1972: 104.

120. Chapter 3.

121. Rhodes 1972: 104–105.

122. Rhodes 1972: 105.

123. Hansen 1991: 255–257; Rhodes 1981: 543–544.

124. Kallet-Marx 1994: 229.

125. Davies 2004: 508; Kallet-Marx 1994: 232–237; Ober 2014; Rhodes 2013: 203–204 n. 3; cf. Cook 1990: 70.

126. Ober 2014.

127. For the *boulē*'s role in aggregating data for the decisions of the *dēmos*, see Ober 2008: 142–159.

128. Kallet-Marx 1994: 236–237; Rhodes 1972: 88; Sommerstein 1981: 184–185.

129. Old comedy generally parodies contemporary political debate (Pritchard 2012a: especially 16, 43–44).

130. Blamire 2001: 114; Davies 2004: 503 n. 41.

131. Kallet-Marx 1994: 232–233.

132. Cook 1990: 95. For the knowledge that the *dēmos* learned by running the democracy, see Ober 2008: 166–167; Pritchard 2010: 33, 47–51.

133. Brock, Geis, and Müller 2006: 202.

134. Ober 2008: 96–97.

135. Kyriazis 2012: 66–67.

136. Chapter 3.

137. Rhodes 1972: 103.

138. Hansen 1991: 152, 157–158.

139. With Rhodes 2013: 217.

140. Rhodes 2013: 218.

141. Rhodes 2013: 218.

142. Cawkwell 1962b plausibly pushes its creation back to the 390s.

143. Rhodes and Osborne 2003: 82–83 *pace* Burke 2005: 31.

2

1. Pinney 1988: 470–471; Shear 2001: 29–38 with primary sources *pace* Neils 1992a: 14–15.

2. Kyle 1987: 33–39, 178–195 and 1992; Shear 2001: 231–387.

3. Johnston 2007.

4. Pinney 1988.

5. For the restoration of this prize, see Shear 2003a: 95.

6. Panathenaic amphorae have been found at Eretria, Sparta, Thebes, and much further afield (Golden 1998: 166; Hodkinson 1999: 152–157; Themelis 2007 with bibliography). E.g., Pind. *Isthm.* 2.19–21, 4.25–26, *Nem.* 4.18–19, *Ol.* 9.88, 13.38–39; cf. *Anth. Pal.* 13.19.1–4 and *IG* ii^2 2313.

7. Shear 2003a: 98.

8. Rhodes 1981: 672–674; Shear 2003a: 96–102.

9. For the testimonia, see Parker 1987: 198–199; Shear 2001: 405.

10. With Hanson 1998: 143–147, 157–161, 236–237.

11. Contrary to what Aristotle and Lysias imply, the collection of olive oil and the production of amphorae certainly did not take place in every year of the Panathenaic quadrennium, as the surviving examples of the mid-fourth century never record the name of the eponymous archon of the first year of this four-year cycle (Valavanis 1997: especially 87).

12. Shear 2001: 455–463.

13. Translated by P. J. Rhodes.

14. For photographs of its two fragments, see Shear 2003a: plates 5 and 6. Neils 1992a: 16, fig. 1 is a photograph of the larger of the two fragments.

15. Shear 2001: 407 and 2003a: 103.

16. Her dissertation collects the archaeological, epigraphical, and literary evidence for the millennium-long history of this festival (Shear 2001). For her new edition of the extant text of *IG* ii² 2311 and her restorations of its lacunae, see Shear 2003a: 88–89 and 103–105 respectively.

17. Shear 2003a: 102. Her figures find some corroboration in Johnston's earlier study of *IG* ii² 2311, which came up with a "possible minimum figure" of 1,423 prize amphorae (1987: 129).

18. Shear 2003a: 102.

19. E.g., Neils 1992b: 39; Pritchett 1956: 195; Valavanis 1986: 455; Young 1984: 116.

20. Bentz 1998: 34; Pritchett 1956: 182.

21. Bentz 1998; cf. Shear 2003a: 101–102.

22. Bentz 1998: 31–40, 200–201.

23. Pritchett 1956: 184; Valavanis 1986: 455 n. 13; Young 1984: 116 n. 13—all with testimonia.

24. So described by Golden 1998: 165.

25. Davison 1958: 31–33; Develin 1984: 133, 136–137; Kyle 1987: 38 n. 31; Shear 2001: 456–458 *pace* Golden 1998: 164–165; Meiggs and Lewis 1969: 236; Rhodes 1981: 669–670.

26. Develin 1984; W. Slater 2007: 32.

27. Shear 2001: 462.

28. This rent is more likely to have replaced rather than supplemented what the city had been spending on this festival (Rhodes and Osborne 2003: 398–403; Shear 2001: 76–83 *pace* Rosivach 1994: 70–72).

29. Tracy 2007: 57.

30. The actual amount of the third known transfer is not preserved (*IG* i³ 378.14–15). P. Wilson likewise writes of the *athlothetai* "regularly" receiving "sums in the region of 10 t. to administer the festival" (2008: 90).

31. For the recorded prices of Attic pots, see Pritchard 1999b: 7 with references.

32. Ceccarelli 2004: 94 n. 9 *pace* Neils 1992a: 16.

33. Shear 2003a: 103–105.

34. Rosivach 1994: 95–96; Tracy 2007: 54—both with testimonia.

35. For these stands for spectators, Ath. 4.167f; Poll. 7.125; Csapo 2007: 104–105; Neils 1992a: 18–20. Postholes dating to the fifth and fourth centuries for these wooden benches have been excavated on both sides of the Panathenaic Way as it traverses the marketplace (Camp 1986: 45–47). For the testimonia for Athena's robe, see Shear 2001: 173–186. Quotation from Shear 2001: 176.

36. Pritchard 2004: 213, 213 n. 27 with primary sources.

37. Csapo and Slater 1994: 146–147; P. Wilson 2000: 89–93.

38. Quotation from Csapo and Slater 1994: 146.

39. Davies 1971: xxi–xxii; P. Wilson 2000: 92 and 2008: 112.

40. Christ 2006: 146–147; Gabrielsen 1994: 124–125; Phillips 1981: 47, Table 5. These figures are 6,000 dr. (Dem. 21.155), 5,300 dr. ([Dem.] 50), 7 trierarchies at 5,143 dr. each (Lys. 21.2), 4,800 dr. (Lys. 32.24, 27), 3 trierarchies at 2,666 dr. each (Lys. 19.29, 42), and 2,000 dr. (Dem. 21.80). *Pace* Gabrielsen 1994: 120–121, the mean of these fourteen figures is 4,436 dr.

41. For example, the speaker of Lysias 21 spent 2,000 dr. on a men's chorus for the Thargelia of 411/0 and more than 1,500 dr. for a boys' chorus at the same festival in 404/3 (1, 4). Similarly a pyrrhic chorus at the Great Panathenaea cost him 800 dr., in 410/9, and 700 dr. at the Small Panathenaea of 404/3.

42. Quotation from P. Wilson 2000: 91; cf. Gabrielsen 1994: 177–178.

43. Even though the *lampadēphoroi* ("torch racers") were drawn from only the upper class (Pritchard 2013: 76–80).

44. Davies 1967: 35–37; Kyle 1987: 190–193. For its staging at the Panathenaic games, see Kyle 1987: 190–191 and 1992: 96; Shear 2001: 335–339. We have no evidence that the torch race at the festival of Pan was tribally organized or liturgically funded (Parker 1996: 163–168 and 2005: 477).

45. Bentz 2007.

46. Christ 2006: 179.

47. Kyle 1987: 193–194 and 1992: 97; Shear 2001: 339–340.

48. Shear 2001: 340.

49. Kyle 1987: 194; Shear 2001: 340 n. 471 *pace* Davies 1967: 39; P. Wilson 2000: 48.

50. Shear 2001: 340–345 and 2003a: 91 n. 11; Kyle 1987: 189–190 and 1992: 94.

51. Agora excavations, Inv. Nos. I 7167, I 7515. For these monuments, see Goette 2007: 120–122.

52. Kyle 1992: 94–95; Shear 2001: 323–331; and especially Ceccarelli 2004.

53. For this mythology, see Shear 2001: 38–42 with primary sources.

54. Davies 1967: 37; Shear 2001: 345–348; P. Wilson 2000: 40. Shear 2003b makes a strong case that the choral victory commemorated by *IG* ii^2 3025 was not associated with the annual Panathenaea.

55. Shear includes this event and the *anthippasia* in her restoration of *IG* ii^2 2311 (2003a: 91, 103–105).

56. E.g., Bentz 2007: 73; Kyle 1992: 94.

57. Shear 2001: 322 and 2003a: 90 with n. 7.

58. E.g., Ceccarelli 2004: 95–99; Davies 1967: 36–37; Pritchard 2005b: 151 n. 47; P. Wilson 2000: 37, 324 n. 137.

59. Ceccarelli 2004: 97.

60. E.g., Parker 2005: 257; Shear 2003a: 91.

61. Gabrielsen 1994: 48.

62. E.g., *IG* ii^2 3025, 3026; *SEG* xxiii.103; Goette 2007: 123–125.

63. Davies 1967: 37; P. Wilson 2000: 37.

64. With Parker 1996: 246 n. 100 and 2005: 479.

65. Crowther 1985; Kyle 1992: 95–96; Shear 2001: 331–334; P. Wilson 2000: 38.

66. Goette 2007: 118–119.

67. Chapter 1.

68. For the regular program of festivals, see, for example, Isae. 9.21; Isoc. 7.29; Lys. 30.19–20. For this belief, see, for example, Isoc. 4.45; [Xen.] *Ath. Pol.* 3.2; cf. Ar. *Nub.* 307–310. Between 120 and 170 days of each year featured a *polis*-sponsored festival or sacrifice in classical Athens (Kyle 2007: 167; Ober 2008: 195–196; and especially Mikalson 1975).

69. On this delight, see Scanlon 1983: 157–158 and 1988: 240, 242.

70. E.g., Aesch. *Sept.* 77, 177–181, 271–278; Hdt. 6.105; cf. *Homeric Hymn to Apollo* 146–150.

71. Mikalson explains clearly the distinction between the festivals, the sacrifices, and the sanctuaries of the *polis* and those of demes and private groups (2005: 160): "We may first distinguish state cults and religious activities from those of a family and village in that they were directed to the welfare of the city-state as a whole, were financed by state revenues, and were open, barring any specific cultic regulations, to all citizens of the city-state and their families. The state at its expense provided through elected, allotted, or appointed officials the sacrificial animals, administered and provided prizes for games, built the temples and other major buildings, and had general over-

sight over the performance of ritual activities. In Athens the priesthoods of most state cults remained with individual families in the fifth century, but the state had lay commissioners to superintend the property, expenses, and even the timely and appropriate performance of the rituals."

72. Humphreys 2004: 85, 94; Parker 2005: 180; Rosivach 1994: 48-60.

73. This is the midpoint of the range of 4 to 10 dr. that Rosivach establishes (1994: 62-63) and dovetails with the 6 to 7 dr. that Jameson works out on the basis of classical and late-antique evidence (1988: 107-112).

74. Rosivach compiles the sales figures of these accounts for each celebration (1994: 50-53). Where more than one sales figure for a festival survives, my calculations employ their average.

75. In spite of its different scale from year to year, the Eleusinia was celebrated annually (Parker 2005: 468-469).

76. Shear 2001: 167-173 with testimonia.

77. This percentage sinks lower if we factor in the 500 goats that the state sacrificed to Artemis Agrotera every year ([Arist.] *Ath. Pol.* 58.1; Ar. *Eq.* 659-662; Xen. *An.* 3.2.12) and the large number of cows it bought for the quadrennial festival on Delos ([Arist.] *Ath. Pol.* 54.7; *IG* ii² 1635.35-36). Against this, the sacrifice of the City Dionysia was probably larger than these accounts suggest, because the sales figure of 306 dr. that it records for 333/2 (*IG* ii² 1496.111-112) is "surprisingly low" in comparison to the 808 dr. of 334/3 and "those for other major festivals elsewhere on the calendar" (Rosivach 1994: 52 n. 109; cf. Csapo and 1994: 113).

78. The sacrifices for Good Fortune and Hermes Hegemonius are first attested in this inscription and hence may have been introduced by the expansion of the festival program that Lycurgus and others championed from the mid-330s (Parker 1996: 231-232, 238 n. 72 and 2005: 456, 473).

79. E.g., Csapo and Slater 1994: no. 141. Csapo 2007: 90-95; Hall 2007: 271; Pickard-Cambridge 1988: 42-47; P. Wilson 2007—all with ancient testimonia.

80. Bruit Zaidman and Schmitt Pantel 1992: 102-108; Parker 2005: 180-183; Phillips and Pritchard 2003: xi-xii; cf. Slater 2007: 21-22.

81. Osborne 1993; Parker 2005: 456-487.

82. Osborne 1993: 25.

83. This applies to four of the five instances in which the accounts record a "*thusia*" for a deity (*IG* ii² 1496.76-77, 84-85, 94-95, 106-107, 115-116, 127-128, 131-132, 140-141). The sacrifice to Zeus the Savior is the exception (88-89, 118-119), as his worship included a *pompē* (Parker 2005: 466-467).

84. Böckh 1828: Volume 1, 281 (Book 2 Chapter 12).

85. For the attested deme and *polis* processions of classical Athens, see Parker 2005: 178 n. 2.

86. For the procession of the City Dionysia, see Csapo and Slater 1994: 105-106, 113-115; Pickard-Cambridge 1988: 61-63. For that of the Great Panathenaea, see Parker 2005: 258-268; Shear 2001: 120-230.

87. Thuc. 6.56.2; Xen. *Eq. Mag.* 3.1-2; Shear 2001: 128-130; Stevenson 2003: 248-251.

88. Shear 2001: 139-143.

89. P. Wilson 2000: 24-25.

90. Fisher 2011: 182.

91. E.g., [Dem.] 50; Lys. 21.1-5; Plut. *Nic.* 3.1-3; Thuc. 6.16.3-4. P. Wilson 2000: 109-197.

92. Christ 2006: 171-184; Dover 1974: 176-177; Ober 1978.

93. Christ 2006: 146-155; Gabrielsen 1994: 43-78; Pritchard 2004: 213-214.

94. Böckh 1828: Volume 2, 205 (Book 3 Chapter 21).

95. Davies 1967: 33.

96. Davies 1967: 40. Of the discrepancy between the actual number of festival liturgies and what this public speaker claimed Davies writes (1967: 40): ". . . one is more or less bound to conclude that either Demosthenes was very badly misinformed or that he was being grossly disingenuous. The latter is much more likely. It suited his case to minimize the extent of the liturgical burden, so that the continuing privileges of the 'twenty or thirty' *ateleis*, on behalf of one of whom (Ktesippus) he was speaking, might appear to be proportionally the less important and the less crippling to Athenian festival finances. The surprising and illuminating thing is that Demosthenes thought he could get away with it."

97. Davies 1967: 39-40 appears to incorporate into its tallies for the 350s the ten liturgies of the Amphiareia (*IG* ii² 417), which was celebrated at the god's sanctuary at Oropus (Parker 2005: 457). Yet it is now better known that Athens lost control of this border region between 366 and the mid-330s (Humphreys 2004: 95, 112-114; Parker 1996: 146-149). Therefore, the proportion of liturgies that the City Dionysia and Great Panathenaea accounted for in the 350s was probably slightly higher than these percentages indicate.

98. My figures are based on Shear's restoration of the prize list (2003a: 103-105).

99. Golden 1998: 104-112; Miller 2004: 13-14.

100. For the Olympic program at the end of the fourth century, see Miller 2003 and 2004: 113-129. For the duration of the Great Panathenaea, see Kyle 2007: 157-158; Shear 2001: 383-384.

101. The staging of such contests at the Olympieia and Theseia is uncertain for this period: there is no evidence that their programs of the hellenistic period date back to the fourth century (Kyle 1987: 40–41, 46; Parker 2005: 477, 483–484).

102. Healey 1990: 1–71; Kyle 1987: 47; Parker 2005: 201–202, 468–469.

103. Clinton 2008: 176–177; Humphreys 2004: 88. These three supervisors were elected by the Athenian *dēmos* (Rhodes 1981: 638). In addition to their sanctuary-based duties, they helped the king archon to run the processions of the Mysteries and the Lenaea ([Arist.] *Ath. Pol.* 57.1; *IG* ii² 1496.74–75, 1672.182).

104. Healey 1990: 18–25, 67 n. 57; Simms 1975: 269–270 *pace* Clinton 1979: 9–12.

105. Parker 1996: 246.

106. [Arist.] *Ath. Pol.* 58.1; Dem. 60.10; Lys. 2.80; cf. Plut. *Per.* 8.6; Kyle 1987: 44–45; Parker 1996: 132 and 2005: 469–470; Pritchett 1985: 106–112; Vanderpool 1969: 3–5. For the common Greek practice of treating the war dead as demigods, see Currie 2005: 89–119.

107. Vanderpool 1969: 1–3.

108. [Arist.] *Ath. Pol.* 54.7; Dem. 19.125; Pind. *Ol.* 9.84–94, *Pyth.* 8.78–79; *IG* i³ 3, 1015 *bis*; Kyle 1987: 46–47; Parker 2005: 473; Vanderpool 1942: 335–336; Woodford 1971: 217.

109. [Arist.] *Ath. Pol.* 54.7; *IG* i³ 375.6–7; ii² 1496.76–77, 98–99, 107–110, 134–135, 138–139; RO 81; cf. *IG* i³ 3 for the ad hoc administration of the Heracleia of the early fifth century.

110. Thessaloniki Archaeological Museum, Inv. No. 5243. The other two were used as funerary urns in Attic cemeteries (Vanderpool 1969: 1–3).

111. The average price of a *medimnos* of wheat was 6 dr. (Pritchett 1956: 196–198 with primary sources).

112. Silver *phialai* weighed between 100 dr. and 200 dr. (D. Harris 1995: s.v. "phiale"; Vickers and Gill 1994: 40–41, 47–52). The maximum cost then is 20 cups at 200 dr. per cup. A second-hand *khalkion thermantērion*, which was a bronze vessel of a similar size to a *lebēs*, sold for 25 dr. 2 ob. at a public auction of the later fifth century (*IG* i³ 421.96). The prize for the individual winner of the torch race at the Great Panathenaea of the 380s was a hydria of an unspecified material, which was worth 30 dr. (*IG* ii² 2311.89). As this was much too much to pay for a finely painted pot (Pritchard 1999b: 7), this prize hydria was presumably made of bronze.

113. My calculations factor in the solitary contests of three other festivals: the torch race on horseback at the Bendideia (Pl. *Resp.* 327a–328b), the foot-

race for youths carrying vine branches at the Oschophoria and the torch race for individuals at the festival of Pan (Hdt. 6.105). We have no evidence concerning their prizes. Kyle 1987: 47–48; Parker 1996: 170–175 and 2005: 211–217, 463, 477.

114. This is borne out as well by the choruses of the City Dionysia and Thargelia: although their *khorēgoi* were appointed at the beginning of the archontic year ([Arist.] *Ath. Pol.* 56.2–3), the training of choruses for Dionysus went on for seven or eight months, whereas the dithyrambic choristers of the Thargelia probably only did so in the two months between the two festivals (Pritchard 2004: 214, 221).

115. Chapter 3.

116. On the Peloponnesian War's eve, the annual public income of Athens was 1,000 t. (Chapter 3). Yet at this time Athens enjoyed significant imperial income and was the center of long-distance trade in the Aegean, while its territory and citizen population were around twenty times larger than an average-sized *polis* (Hansen 2006a: 77–84; Hansen and Nielsen 2004: 70–73). Thus, its annual income would have been higher by an order of magnitude than the vast majority of Greek city-states.

117. E.g., Boedeker and Raaflaub 1998; Dawson 1995: 4–5; Despotopoulos 1996; Ober 2008: 81–82; Pritchard 2007b: 331–332 and 2010: 4–5. *Contra* Samons 2001.

118. For the competition-driven innovations in these four genres see respectively Burian 1997: 206; Bremer 1993: 160–165; Seaford 1984: 44; and Zimmermann 1993: 53–54.

119. Pritchard 2013: 14–16.

120. For these judges, see Csapo and Slater 1994: 157–165.

121. Revermann 2006: 113–115.

122. Camp 2001: 74–82.

123. Boersma 1970: 70.

124. Stanier 1953: especially 73. These estimates are still widely accepted (e.g., Cook 1990: 94 n. 91; Kallet 1998: 48). Stanier erroneously saw the gold of Athena's chryselephantine statue as a cost to the public purse (Stanier 1953: 69). In classical Athens, gold was fourteen times more valuable by weight than silver (*IG* i³ 458.15–18; Dinsmoor 1937: 509–510). Thus, the 40 t. of gold in this statue was worth 560 t. But this was still counted by the Athenians as part of their cash reserves (Thuc. 2.13.5) and hence was not an expense. The statue thus "functioned as a kind of emergency savings account" (Cook 1990: 94). The Athenians had simply converted 560 t. of their public wealth into a less liquid form.

125. Boersma 1970: 65–96; Camp 2001: 72–117. This is John Camp's tally (2001: 117).

126. Boersma 1970: 84, 89. For the war's cost, see Chapter 4.

127. Camp 2001: 117.

128. Camp 2001: 90–100, 104–105, 117–137.

129. Boersma 1970: 177, 179.

130. Camp 2001: 137–144.

131. Chapter 1.

132. Camp 2001: 144–160.

133. Rhodes 2013: 206.

134. In so doing, Böckh took Plut. *Per.* 12 at face value (1828: Volume 1, 268–269 [Book 2 Chapter 10]).

135. Kallet-Marx 1989: 252–253.

3

1. [Arist.] *Ath. Pol.* 27.1–4; Arist. *Pol.* 1274a8–9; Pl. *Grg.* 515e; Plut. *Per.* 9.1–3. It is more likely that he did so after rather than before Cimon's ostracism in 462/1 (Fornara and Samons 1991: 25–26; Loomis 1998: 9–10; Rhodes 1981: 339–340, 690).

2. On Ar. *Av.* 1541, *Ran.* 140, *Vesp.* 88, 300.

3. Cook 1990: 84; Loomis 1998: 15 n. 19; Sommerstein 1981: 147; Todd 1993: 88. *Contra* Rosivach 2010: 148–149 n. 20.

4. Cook 1990: 76; Hansen 1991: 188.

5. Böckh 1828: Volume 1, 311 (Book 2 Chapter 15); Hansen 1979a: 243; Rhodes 1981: 657.

6. Cook 1990: 94 *pace* Unz 1985: 26–27.

7. Mikalson 1975.

8. Hansen 1991: 196.

9. Hansen 1979a: 245 and 1991: 186; Rhodes 1981: 657–658.

10. Hansen 1979a: 246.

11. Hansen 1979a: 244.

12. Hansen 1979a: 244; cf. 1991: 186.

13. Hansen 1991: 183.

14. Hansen 1979b: 7; Sommerstein 1983: 200.

15. Hansen 1991: 187.

16. Hansen 1991: 183.

17. Hansen 1991: 187 *pace* Rhodes 1981: 714–715.

18. Hansen estimates their wages at between 22 and 37 t. per year (1991: 189, 255).

19. Böckh 1828: Volume 1, 315-316 (Book 2 Chapter 15).

20. Marr and Rhodes 2008: 90-91; Meiggs 1972: 212-233.

21. For this dating of Pseudo-Xenophon's treatise, see Marr and Rhodes 2008: 3-6; Osborne 2004: 5-19, both with bibliography.

22. Todd 1993: 148-149, which is the source of the quotation.

23. Marr and Rhodes 2008: 157.

24. P. J. Rhodes has pointed out to me that another reason for supposing this is the system of arbitration that Athens set up at the beginning of the fourth century. This required the two sides in most private lawsuits to attempt to find a resolution with the help of an arbitrator (Hansen 1991: 192, 197; Harrison 1971: 66-68; Rhodes 1981: 591). One or both sides could proceed to a jury court only if this arbitration failed ([Arist.] *Ath. Pol.* 53.2). Without such a system, the lawcourts of the 420s would have heard many more private cases.

25. With Rosivach 2010: 145-148.

26. Hansen 1979b: 7; A. H. M. Jones 1957: 136-137 n. 10.

27. Gomme, Andrewes, and Dover 1981: 181; Hansen 1979b: 7; Rhodes 1981: 692 *pace* Rosivach 2010: 148 n. 18.

28. Hansen 1991: 250.

29. Hansen 1991: 253; Rhodes 1972: 39.

30. Blamire 2001: 115-116.

31. Chapter 4.

32. Sinclair 1988: 66 n. 84 *pace* Loomis 1998: 20.

33. This assumption, which is widely made (e.g., Hansen 1979b: 15-16; Rosivach 2011: 182), seems reasonable, even though the first testimony for the restoration of this *misthos* comes from 353/2 (Dem. 24.97).

34. Hansen 1991: 250-251.

35. With Rhodes 1981: 521.

36. Hansen 1991: 253.

37. Wealthy Athenians usually had a house in or near their ancestral deme and another in the city or the Piraeus (Osborne 1985, 47-50, 69, with ancient testimonia).

38. Hansen 1991: 248-249. For the most part, they performed this service only once in their lives.

39. Hansen 1991: 309, which is the source of the quotation.

40. Hansen 1991: 255. *Contra* Sinclair 1988: 112-114.

41. Hansen costs it at "about 15 t." (1991: 255, 315-316).

42. Hansen 1987: 46-47; Sommerstein 1998: 174; Yakobson 2011: 140.

43. Burke 2005: 37; Hansen 1991: 150; Loomis 1998: 20-22; Stockton 1990: 53, 72.

44. For the date of the *Assemblywomen* of Aristophanes, see Sommerstein 1998: 1.

45. But I am not convinced by Gauthier's larger argument that the desire for such punctuality was the only reason why the Athenians introduced assembly pay (1993: 241, 247-249).

46. Loomis 1998: 25-26.

47. Chapter 1.

48. Hansen 1991: 150.

49. Gauthier 1993: 239-240; Hansen 1986b: 94.

50. Gauthier 1993: 246-247; Rhodes 1981: 491.

51. Hansen 1991: 94-97, 130 with bibliography.

52. Hansen 1976; 1986b: 94; 1987: 47; and 1991: 130 *pace* A. H. M. Jones 1957: 6; Sinclair 1988: 114-119.

53. Hansen 1991: 133; Rhodes 1981: 521-522.

54. Pritchard 2010: 57-58.

55. Rhodes 1972: 104; Sommerstein 1998: 146.

56. Hansen 1991: 150, 315-316.

57. In this chapter as elsewhere, the treatise's author uses *trophē, eis sitēsis*, and cognate words as synonyms for *misthos* (Gabrielsen 1981: 67-81, 151-155; cf. Loomis 1998: 26 n. 60).

58. Hansen 1980b: 166 and 1991: 240; A. H. M. Jones 1957: 136 n. 9.

59. Hansen 1980b: 155-156; cf. A. H. M. Jones 1957: 6, 136 n. 9; Rhodes 1981: 305.

60. E.g., French 1964: 150; A. H. M. Jones 1957: 136 n. 9, which is the source of the quotation; Rhodes 1981: 304-305.

61. Hansen 1979b: 12 and 1980b: 151; Rhodes 1981: 305; Rosivach 2010: 148 n. 18; cf. Meiggs 1972: 215 n. 1.

62. Pritchard 2010: 20-21.

63. Pritchard 2010: 19; Spence 1993: 9-17 and 2010: 119-120.

64. Hansen 1979b: 12-14. For its new date, see Rhodes 2008: 501, 505 and 2009: 4.

65. Cook 1990: 71-72; Rosivach 2011: 176-178.

66. Rhodes 1981: 25, 301-302; Rosivach 2011: 178.

67. Hansen 1980b; cf. 1991: 240.

68. Hansen 1980b: 156-162; cf. Gabrielsen 1981: 64-65.

69. Hansen 1980b: 163-165.

70. Aleshire 1994; Ostwald 1986: 137-174.

71. Hansen 1980b: 165.

72. For its date and that of *IG* i³ 1453, B/G, see Rhodes 2008: 501, 503. Both decrees refer to "the *arkhontes* in the cities." I follow the majority view in seeing them as Athenian, not local, magistrates (e.g., Balcer 1976: 273; Meiggs 1972: 213–214; Meritt, Wade-Gery, and McGregor 1950: 144–145; Samons 2000: 192–193). *Contra* Leppin 1992.

73. Balcer 1976: 269, 273; Meiggs 1972: 213.

74. Balcer 1976: 260, 285; Meiggs 1972: 212.

75. E.g., Balcer 1976: 285; Meiggs 1972: 215.

76. Hansen 1991: 237–238.

77. Meiggs 1972: 215.

78. Balcer 1976; Finley 1978: 108–109, 120; Meiggs 1972: 212–215; Meritt, Wade-Gery, and McGregor 1950: 146; Podlecki 1998: 167; Samons 2000: 193.

79. Hansen 1979b: 14–19; 1980a; 1980b: 167; 1987: 98; 1991: 240–242.

80. Hansen 1979b: 13 and 1991: 240–241.

81. Hansen 1979b: 14 (which is the source of the quotation), 15; cf. Mac-Dowell 1983: 76.

82. Hansen 1991: 241, 300–304; cf. Phillips 2012: 101–102.

83. Hansen 1979b: 18.

84. Hansen 1980a: 124.

85. See, respectively, RO 81.12–13, *IG* ii² 1672.255–258 and [Arist.] *Ath. Pol.* 62.2.

86. Hansen 1980a: 111–119 and 1991: 241–242.

87. Hansen 1980a: 124 and 1991: 241.

88. Hansen 1980a: 125.

89. Hansen 1980a: 106–113.

90. Hansen 1979b: 22 n. 46; Rhodes 1981: 695.

91. He published Gabrielsen 1981 when he was an undergraduate student. Hansen managed to publish his response (1980a) before that book's appearance.

92. Lewis (1982: 269) and MacDowell (1983: 76) backed Hansen in their reviews of Gabrielsen 1981. In their reviews of the same book, Cawkwell (1983: 839) and Stroud (1982: 158) sided with Gabrielsen, with the latter describing Gabrielsen's belief in *misthos* for fourth-century magistrates as "the majority view." Cartledge (1982) and Möller (2007: 380) avoided taking sides.

93. For example, Burke (2005: 34) and Loomis (1998: 182 n. 34) back Gabrielsen, while Rosivach (2011: 182 n. 34) and Taylor (2001a: 57) support Hansen. Rhodes (2013: 206) and Gabrielsen (2013: 333) have remained steadfast in their rejection of Hansen's position.

94. *Pace* Taylor 2001a: 57.

95. In their own refutations Gabrielsen (1981) and Rhodes (1981: 695) canvassed these three reasons to varying extents. Gabrielsen touched on the first only in passing and did not develop fully the second. He was immensely strong on the third. Rhodes dealt briefly with the second only.

96. Chapter 1.

97. Taylor 2001b: 159.

98. E.g., Aeschin. 1.106, 110–113; Dem. 24.14, 112; Lys. 27.2–3, 6–8; 28.3–4; Xen. *Eq. Mag.* 1.10.

99. Taylor 2001b: 160.

100. Gabrielsen 1981: 100; Rhodes 1981: 598.

101. Hamel 1998: 122.

102. Rhodes 1972: 111–113; Taylor 2001b: 154–157.

103. Hamel 1998: 122–123; Hansen 1991: 220–221; Rhodes 1981: 540–541.

104. Hansen 1991: 221–222.

105. Hansen 1991: 221; Rhodes 1981: 540–541.

106. Hamel 1998: 126–130; Hansen 1991: 222–224.

107. For the elite's purchasing of such lessons, see Pritchard 2013: 5, 46, 107.

108. Christ 2006: 61; Taylor 2001a: 61–64.

109. Hansen 1983: 42 with n. 32.

110. Kamen 2013: 100; Pritchard 2013: 8.

111. Hansen 1991: 222–223.

112. For this role of *aiskhunē* in regulating Athenian behavior, see Balot 2010: 101–103.

113. For the *atimia* of public debtors, see Dem. 59.6.

114. Gabrielsen 1994: 116, 250 n. 25.

115. Cook 1990: 75; Gabrielsen 2007: 268–271.

116. Hamel 1998: 158 *pace* Taylor 2001a: 61.

117. E.g., Dem. 24.11–14; Lys. 28.1–4, 6, 10; 29.2, 5, 8–11, 14; Xen. *Hell.* 1.2.4–5; Gabrielsen 2007: 255–256.

118. Burckhardt 1995: 115, 130; Burke 2005: 35; Hamel 1998: 44–46; Millett 1993: 190 and 2009: 475; Pritchett 1971: 87–90.

119. Frölich 2000.

120. Hamel 1998: 130–132; Hansen 1991: 216–218.

121. Hansen 1991: 212–215.

122. Hamel 1998: 132, 136.

123. Hamel 1998: 118; E. M. Harris 2010: 411.

124. Hamel 1998: 148.

125. Hamel 1998: 135, 155; E. M. Harris 2010: 412.

126. Rhodes 1981: 573–574.

127. Translated by P. J. Rhodes.

128. For this consumption of the elite, see Pritchard 2013: 4–5, 130–133.

129. For the duties of the *agoranomoi*, see Ar. *Ach.* 724, 968; [Arist.] *Ath. Pol.* 51.1; Dem. 57.31, 34; Rhodes 1981: 575–576. For the treasurers of Athena, see [Arist.] *Ath. Pol.* 47.1, 60.3; Gabrielsen 1981: 145 n. 114; Hansen 1980a: 121; Rhodes 1981: 575–576. For the *basileus*, see [Arist.] *Ath. Pol.* 57; Rhodes 1981: 636–650.

130. For this participation of the poor, see Gabrielsen 1981: 111–119.

131. Chapter 1.

132. Gabrielsen 1981: 118–119; A. H. M. Jones 1957: 18; Stroud 1982: 158.

133. Gabrielsen 1981: 88–108.

134. Kennedy 1985: 512–513.

135. For his antidemocratic argument, see Ober 1998: 277–282.

136. For the classical elite's responsibility for liturgies, see Chapter 2.

137. Fourth-century writers quite frequently used *lemma* as a synonym of *misthos* for political participation (e.g., Arist. *Pol.* 1318b15–16; Dem. 3.34; Isoc. 8.130, 15.152).

138. It clearly is a view that dates back to the previous century (e.g., [Xen.] *Ath. Pol.* 1.13).

139. Pritchard 2013: 19–20, 113, 160.

140. Ober 1998: 249, 254–255.

141. For examples, see Hansen 1980a: 120 n. 36.

142. Hansen 1980a: 120 and 1991: 232–233.

143. Gabrielsen 1981: 119–146.

144. E. M. Harris 2013: 387–400.

145. The exception is the defense speech of Andocides in which he claims that his accusers actually used to propose him to be a liturgist (*lēitourgein houtoi prouballonto*), because the catalogue that he gives as support of this claim includes not just two festival liturgies but also his service as a *tamias* of sacred funds on the Acropolis (7.132). The characterization of this treasurership as liturgy was probably a self-serving exaggeration on the part of Andocides (cf. Isoc. 16.32–33). What helped him to get away with it was that such positions appear to have been among the democracy's most demanding. This is suggested by the regular inability of the Athenians, in both centuries, to find enough candidates to fill the board in charge of Athena's money (Gabrielsen 1981: 145 n. 114).

146. Kennedy 1985: 512; Ober 1998: 256.

147. For this procedure, see Christ 1990.

148. Gabrielsen 1981: 96–97.

149. Hansen 1979b: 7–11, 13 and 1991: 241.

150. See the first three sections of this chapter, above.

151. Chapter 1.

152. As the *epistatai* of the Eleusinian sanctuary, for example, could have easily taken their *misthos* from the sacred funds that they managed, the payment of them by the *kōlakretai* looks significant (Clinton 2008: 53; Meritt, Wade-Gery, and McGregor 1950: 360–361). The Athenians had the *kōlakretai* pay them out of secular funds probably to minimize the chances of financial malfeasance or, at least, the appearance of it. *Pace* D. M. Lewis 1982: 269, this would explain why we do not find *misthos* for *arkhontes* managing sacred funds in the building accounts of the Erechtheum in the late fifth century or in the accounts of the Eleusinian sanctuary in the later part of the next century (see below).

153. Rosivach 2010: 148 n. 18.

154. Loomis 1998: 25, 101.

155. Clinton 2008: 184, 187; Loomis 1998: 25, 101–102.

156. Loomis 1998: 99.

157. A. H. M. Jones 1957: 6; Loomis 1998: 10; Rosivach 2010: 148 n. 18.

158. E.g., Gabrielsen 1981: 148; Hansen 1979b: 11; A. H. M. Jones 1957: 5.

159. Hansen 1980b: 167.

160. Chapter 1.

161. Here Rhodes 1981 is indispensible.

162. *Pace* Gabrielsen 1981: 148.

163. Hansen 1980b: 156–162.

164. Chapter 4.

165. *Pace* A. H. M. Jones 1957: 6, which costs this form of remuneration at 21 t. per year.

166. Chapter 1.

167. Loomis 1998: 9–31.

168. Loomis 1998: 11–12.

169. E.g., Böckh 1828: Volume 1, 318 (Book 2 Chapter 16); Meiggs 1972: 586; Samons 2000: 193 n. 89; Sommerstein 1987: 268; cf. Balcer 1976: 261.

170. Chapter 4.

171. See, for example, Dem. 19.70, 249; Antiph. 6.49; Lys. 30.29; *IG* i³ 476.61–62, 268–269.

172. Hansen 1991: 224–225; Robb 1994: 137–138.

173. A. H. M. Jones 1957: 18.

174. Pritchard 2012a: 36.

175. For the dates of these two speeches, see Kennedy 1985: 520–521.

176. Hansen 1980a: 160.

177. For the social background of, for example, generals, see Hansen 1991: 268–271. For the elite's education, see Pritchard 2013: 34–83.

178. The figures are 5 ob. per day from the Erechtheum accounts of 408/7 (*IG i³* 476.61–62, 268–269; Loomis 1998: 99; Randall 1953: 208), a restored 3 ob. per day from the Eleusinian accounts of—possibly—333/2 (Loomis 1998: 25, 101), and 1 ob. per day from the Eleusinian accounts of 329/8 (*IG* ii2 1672.12, 43–44, 118–119, 143). The 2 to 3 dr. per month or prytany that Demosthenes implies (19.200) is an "absurdly low figure" (Loomis 1998: 23), which cannot be used in this calculation.

179. Hansen does not attempt a cost estimate of undersecretaries (1991: 244–245).

180. Fisher 1993: 55–57; Hansen 1991: 123–124; Kamen 2013: 25–27; Lewis 1990: 254–258.

181. Hansen 1991: 123. Lewis wrote too (1990: 257): "My feeling is that it would be conservative to suggest that the Athenian state owned several hundred slaves in the fourth century, and that there would be nothing particularly surprising if the total ran into four figures."

182. Meritt and Traill 1974: no. 72 and cf. nos. 37 and 62; *SEG* xxiv.165; [Arist.] *Ath. Pol.* 47.5; Traill 1969.

183. Rhodes 1981: 707 *pace* Lewis 1990: 255.

184. Stroud 1974.

185. With C. P. Jones 1987.

186. Cook 1990: 84; Loomis 1998: 113–134.

187. Hansen 1980b: 163–165.

188. Jacob 1928: 147–150.

189. A. H. M. Jones 1957: 80–81.

190. Hansen 1986a: 9–11.

191. Coale and Demeny 1966.

192. E.g., Hansen 1986, 1988, 2006b, and 2006c.

193. Hansen 1986: 11–12.

194. Coale and Demeny 1966: 128.

195. For the positive reception of Hansen's demography, see Golden 2000; Osborne 1987.

196. I remain indebted to Martin Bell and Philipp Ueffing of the University of Queensland for this table's figures.

197. Pritchett 1956: 276–281 and 1961.

198. Pritchett 1956: 276.

199. For this corps, see Hunter 1994: 145–149; Lissarrague 1990: 125–127; Trundle 2010: 149–152; Yakobson 2011: 139–142.

200. This is the number that Aeschines and Andocides give.

201. Jacob 1928: 64–73.

202. Jacob 1928: 69.

203. Hansen 1991: 124; Jacob 1928: 69; Yakobson 2011: 141 *pace* Hall 2006: 233; A. H. M. Jones 1957: 18; Plassart 1913: 188.

204. Hall 2006: 234.

205. Lissarrague 1990: 125–126.

206. With Trundle 2010: 151–152.

207. *Pace* Böckh 1828: Volume 1, 277–279 (Book 2 Chapter 11) and Plassart 1913: 188–189, which cost this corps at close to 40 t. a year.

208. Hansen 1991: 137; Rhodes 1972: 146–147.

209. E.g., Hunter 1994: 147–148; Jacob 1928: 76–78; Plassart 1913: 195. *Contra* Hansen 1991: 124.

210. E. M. Harris 2000: 60–67; Henry 1983: 22–38.

211. Henry 1983: 22.

212. P. Wilson 2009.

213. Lambert 2004: 86; 2012: 176.

214. E.g., *IG* ii² 103.27–30, 207a.7–8, 223.A9–13, 330.61–62, 338.19–21, 354.21–23; RO 64.26–29.

215. Hansen 1987: 115.

216. Lambert 2012: 177.

217. Chapter 1.

218. Hansen 1987: 114–115.

219. Hansen 1987: 187 n. 735.

220. Hansen 1987: 115 and 1991: 316.

221. In Lambert's study of honorary decrees for Athenians from 352/1 to 322/1 there are only twelve that award gold crowns (2004: 88–89, 105–111).

222. Hansen 1987: 187 n. 737; Henry 1983: 24; Lambert 2004: 105.

223. Hansen 1987: 115.

224. *IG* ii² 103 of 369/8, for example, gives several crowns to foreigners (26–30); *IG* ii² 207a of c. 361/0, one crown (7–8); and RO 64 of 347/6, three crowns, while also noting one more crown earlier (27–29).

225. Böckh estimated the cost of such honors at 2 to 3 t. per year (1828: Volume 1, 329 [Book 2 Chapter 18]).

226. Thus, Burke's estimate of 125 to 150 t. for the fifth-century democracy and Kallet's estimate of 75 t. are too low (Burke 2005: 12, 27; Kallet 1998: 46).

227. Chapter 2.

228. Chapter 4.

229. Blamire 2001: 106–107; Meritt, Wade-Gery, and McGregor 1950: 333.

230. Meritt, Wade-Gery, and McGregor 1950: 345.

231. Chapter 2.

232. Chapter 4.

233. *Pace* Hansen 1976: 133–134; 1987: 48; and 1991: 318–319.

234. By the late 370s the members of the Second Athenian League were paying *suntaxeis* or contributions (Chapter 4). But Athens was not free to spend this external income as it saw fit, as had been the case with the *phoros* (Rhodes 2006: 233), for it was this league's independent council that voted on how much members should pay and how the income so raised could be spent (RO 52.9–12, 72.25–26).

4

1. Cook 1990: 91; Gabrielsen 2007: 263.

2. Gomme 1956: Volume 1, 17–19; Meritt, Wade-Gery, and McGregor 1950: 334; Samons 2000: 200–206, 309.

3. E.g., *IG* i³ 375.4, 8, 9–10, 12, 16–18, 24; 464.105–106; 465.123–125, 127–128; 466.144–145. Meritt, Wade-Gery, and McGregor 1950: 329–332; Samons 2000: 230.

4. Blamire 2001: 106.

5. Kallet 1998: 44, 46.

6. Chapters 2 and 3.

7. Gomme 1956: Volume 2, 19. In the next century the use of the city's surplus income on warmaking was standard practice until the creation of the so-called festival fund by 349/8 at the latest (Chapter 1).

8. Rhodes 2006: 92–93.

9. Böckh 1828: Volume 1, 386–387 (Book 2 Chapter 24); Brun 1983: 22–26; Christ 2006: 161–162; Hornblower 1991: 403–404; Samons 2000: 205.

10. Brun 1983: 24; Meritt, Wade-Gery, and McGregor 1950: 345; West 1930: 238 *pace* Burke 2005: 24; Gomme 1956: Volume 2, 279.

11. Meiggs 1972: 325; Meiggs and Lewis 1969: 193–194; Meritt, Wade-Gery, and McGregor 1950: 345.

12. Sommerstein 1983: 197.

13. Meritt, Wade-Gery, and McGregor 1950: 345.

14. Blamire 2001: 103–105; Samons 2000: 107–163.

15. This inscription is ML 72. Gomme 1956: volume 2, 432–436.

16. Meiggs and Lewis 1969: 217; West 1930: 233–236.

17. Meritt, Wade-Gery, and McGregor 1950: 341–345.

18. E.g., Blamire 2001: 109; Jacquemin 2000: 149–150; Samons 2000: 209.

19. As is widely assumed; see, for example, Blamire 2001: 109; Cook 1990:

89; Gabrielsen 1994: 116 and 2007: 265; Meiggs and Lewis 1969: 216; Samons 2000: 209; van Wees 2000: 107-108.

20. E.g., Andoc. 3.7-9; Thuc. 2.24.1; Xen. *An.* 7.1.27, *Vect.* 5.12. Gauthier 1976: 213.

21. For the number of ships in the expeditions of these years and their approximate number of days at sea, see Rosivach 1985 (1992): 45-47. At the daily rate of 1 dr. per combatant, the 200-strong crew of a trireme cost 1 t. per month (e.g., Thuc. 6.8.1).

22. For public building during the Archidamian War, see Chapter 2.

23. For this view of Athenian war finance, see, for example, Meiggs and Lewis 1969: 216; Meritt, Wade-Gery, and McGregor 1950: 329-332; Rhodes 1988: 194; Samons 2000: 23, 162. Quotation from Meiggs and Lewis 1969: 216.

24. *Pace* Cook 1990: 89 and Kallet 1998: 46.

25. Chapter 1.

26. Chapter 2.

27. For the fleet sizes of these years, see Amit 1965: 22-23; Böckh 1828: Volume 1, 354-355 (Book 2 Chapter 21); Rosivach 1985 (1992): 44-51.

28. For Pericles and financial resources, see Thuc. 1.142.4-5; 1.143.4-5; 2.13.2-3; 2.65.7. For this strategic thinking of the *dēmos*, see, for example, Andoc. 3; Ar. *Ach.* 162-163, *Av.* 378-380, *Ran.* 365, *Lys.* 170-176, 421-423, 488, 496, *Plut.* 112; Dem. 4.40, 8.48, 9.40, 9.70-72, 13.10, 22.12-17; Lys. 13.46-48, 28.15; *IG* ii² 1604.70, 1607b.22, 47, 62; Gabrielsen 2008: 60-61; Pritchard 1998: 55 and 1999a: 214-222.

29. Blamire 2001: 113; Samons 2000: 166-167.

30. Blamire 2001: 114; Samons 2000: 235.

31. Loomis 1998: 44-45.

32. Bugh 1988: 82-85.

33. With Loomis 1995.

34. Bugh 1988: 221.

35. E.g., Austin and Vidal-Naquet 1977: 135-138; Brun 1983: 143-144, 176-177, 183-185; Davies 1978: 198-199; de Ste. Croix 1981: 293, 607 n. 37; Ehrenberg 1951: 314-317; Mossé 1962: 315-322; Samons 2004: 143-162. For useful critiques of this decline historiography, see Burckhardt 1995: 108-110; Harding 1988: 61 and 1995: 105-106; Millett 1993—all with bibliography.

36. Mader 2006; Roisman 2005: 115-156.

37. Pritchard 2010: 6; Roisman 2005: 117-118—both with primary sources.

38. While his audience would have interpreted the shirking of military service as cowardice anyway (e.g., Eur. *Heracl.* 700-701; *Phoen.* 999-1005), Demosthenes repeatedly says that they are cowards (e.g., 3.31-32, 36; 4.42).

39. For the lack of political success of Demosthenes before the mid 340s and the strategic shortcomings of his military proposals, see Badian 2000: 26-37; Cawkwell 1962a: 135-140, 1962b: 377-378, and 1963: 53.

40. Pritchard 2010: 51-55.

41. E.g., Cawkwell 1963: 53. Burckhardt 1995: 129-133 and 1996: 211-229.

42. Burckhardt 1995 and 1996: 76-153. Quotation from Burckhardt 1995: 128.

43. E.g., Dem. 8.9, 23.113; [Dem.] 50.21-22; Isoc. 15.111-112; Xen. *Hell.* 4.5.11-18.

44. Burckhardt 1995: 118-120; Hanson 2000; Harding 1995: 11-12; Lonis 1979: 17-21.

45. Burckhardt 1995: 120-126.

46. Austin 1994: 528; Cawkwell 1962b: 383.

47. Burckhardt 1995: 112; Cawkwell 1984; Harding 1988: 68-71; Heskel 1997: 137. Quotation from Cawkwell 1984: 342.

48. Blanshard 2010; Pritchard 2010: 47-51, 53-54.

49. For this revival of Athenian imperialism, see Seager 1967.

50. For the extent to which Athens kept these promises, see especially Cargill 1981: 129-160.

51. Cook 1990: 71, 77; Figueira 1998: 261-263; Gabrielsen 1994: 118-119.

52. Cawkwell 1984: 334; Heskel 1997: 144; Roisman 2005: 125-127.

53. Burckhardt 1995: 125; Cawkwell 1984: 338-339; Gabrielsen 1994: 105-110 *pace* Amit 1965: 48-49. For the fifth-century situation, see Pritchard 2000: 112-114.

54. Roisman 2005: 125-126.

55. For the reform of the *eisphora* and its regular levying in the fourth century, see Austin 1994: 546-548; Brun 1983: 28-73; Christ 2006: 147-149, 165-166; Gabrielsen 2013: 342. For the *suntaxeis*, which were probably first paid in the late 370s, see Austin 1994: 552; Brun 1983: 91-93; Cargill 1981: 124-128; Gabrielsen 2007: 267-268.

56. Gabrielsen 1994: 182-199.

57. For the regular use of this surplus for war before the creation of the festival fund by 349/8 at the latest, see Chapter 1. For these Persian gifts, see Diod. Sic. 6.22.1; Lys. 19.24-26; Xen. *Hell.* 4.4.2; Austin 1994: 556-557; Heskel 1997: 44, 124-125.

58. Gabrielsen 1994: 116, 150 n. 25.

59. Chapter 3.

60. *Pace* Robbins 1918: 362-363, 378, 385.

61. Gabrielsen 1994: 118.

62. Brun 1983: 154–158; Robbins 1918: 378–386; C. H. Wilson 1970: 305–308.

63. E.g., Blackman 1969: 213–214; Böckh 1828: Volume 1, 333 (Book 2 Chapter 19); Robbins 1918: 368.

64. Gabrielsen 1994: 134–136, 2007: 261, and 2008: 51–52; Meiggs and Lewis 1969: 279–280; Rhodes 1972: 115–117.

65. Gabrielsen 1994: 135–136.

66. Rhodes 1972: 117–119; Rhodes and Osborne 2003: 522.

67. Brun 1983: 145–146; Sinclair 1978: 50–51; C. H. Wilson 1970: 309–311.

68. Sinclair 1978: especially 51–52.

69. *IG* ii² 1606.11–12, 24–26, 29–30, 69–70, 74–80, 78–79, 82–83, 86–88; 1607.4, 7–8, 17, 20–21, 44, 114–115, 138–140, 142–143, 145–146, 152–153; 1608.5; 1610.23–24, 30–32. The other accounts of this decade also list the ships that the Thebans as new allies gave the Athenians (1605.13–14; 1607.155–156).

70. *IG* ii² 1609 has several "new" ships (97, 99–100, 102), but this inscription could equally be from 366/5 or 371/0.

71. Böckh 1828: Volume 1, 145–146 (Book 1 Chapter 19); Robbins 1918: 363–364; cf. Unz 1985: 36 n. 57.

72. Böckh 1840: 220; Brun 1983: 143; Christ 2006: 175; Gabrielsen 1994: 139, 142–143.

73. Gabrielsen 2008: 49–51.

74. Gabrielsen 1994: 152–153—with primary sources.

75. Bugh 1988: 56–57; Pritchard 2010: 48–49; Spence 1993: 183, 279 and 2010: 113–114.

76. Braun 1970: 129–132, 198–269; Kroll 1977.

77. Kroll 1977: 97–100.

78. Spence 1993: 274–277. The mean of the five hundred or so tablets of the next century is 676 dr. Since the third-century cavalry was considerably smaller and more socially exclusive, its members could afford more expensive warhorses (277–278).

79. Bugh 1988: 62–74, 158.

80. Kroll 1977: 93–99.

81. Bugh 1988: 154–156; Hansen 1991: 316.

82. Brun 1983: 147–148; Gabrielsen 2007: 258 and 2008: 60.

83. Frederiksen 2011: 100.

84. Gabrielsen 2013: 334.

85. I thank Stephen C. Todd for drawing this passage to my attention.

86. Kroll 1977: 97–98 n. 36; Loomis 1998: 51.

87. Stroud 1971: 297–301.

88. With Loomis 1995.

89. Loomis 1998: 45–46.

90. For most of the classical period, Athenian authors employed *misthos* to describe the sum of military pay and any other monies handed out for maintenance in the field (Cook 1990: 78–79; Loomis 1998: 33–36, 49). This changes only in the late 350s when a distinction emerges between the *sitēresion* ("maintenance money") that generals handed out and *misthos* that was over and above this (e.g., [Dem.] 50.10).

91. Spence 1993: 280–285.

92. E.g., Robbins 1918: 378.

93. Hansen 1991: 316.

94. E.g., Dem. 4.34, 8.29; Thuc. 3.33.1, 3.77.3, 6.53.1, 6.61.4, 8.74.1; Xen. *Hell.* 6.2.14; Brun 1983: 149–150; Gabrielsen 1994: 73, 243 n. 12.

95. It was most probably restored to 1 dr. per sailor per day or 1 t. per trireme crew per month (Loomis 1998: 57–58).

96. Brun 1983: 150–151; Robbins 1918: 373–376; C. H. Wilson 1970: 313–314.

97. Translated by Brownson.

98. Brun 1983: 151.

99. For the public support of the orphans, see Lys. fr. VI.35–40 Gernet and Bizos; Pl. *Menex.* 248e–249b; Thuc. 2.46.1; Böckh 1828: 327–328 (Book 2 Chapter 17); Hansen 1991: 98. *Pace* Stroud 1971: 289, Aeschin. 3.153–155 and Isoc. 8.82–83 do not show that Athens stopped this support in the fourth century. They attest only to there no longer being an armed parade of orphans at the City Dionysia.

100. Around 400 BC war orphans were paid 1 ob. each per day (Loomis 1998: 223–234).

101. Pritchard 2013: 162.

102. For their number, see Pritchard 2013: 79.

103. Hansen 1991: 316.

104. Friend 2009: 4–56; Sommerstein 1997: 53–59. *Contra* Barringer 2001: 47–53; Winkler 1990: 26–31.

105. Robbins 1918: 378–386.

106. Christ 2006: 152.

107. Loomis 1998: 57–58.

108. Chapter 1.

109. Heskel 1997: 15–17.

110. Cawkwell 1984: 334–335—with primary sources.

111. Cawkwell 1984: 334. E.g., Burckhardt 1995: 122.

112. *Pace* Dem. 9.50–51.

113. Heskel 1997: 22–26, 40–46.

114. Heskel 1997: 26–37, 43–52, 134–153.

115. Heskel 1997: 85–88, 141–142.

116. Heskel 1997: 54–60.

117. The exceptions were the *Paralus* and the *Salaminia*, whose crews were paid year round (see "The Full Cost of the Armed Forces in the 370s," above).

118. The cost of the two messenger ships alone was 25 t. 1,620 dr.

119. This is simply the sum of the 102 ships of 377/6 and the documented net gains from the subsequent sea battles of the 370s (see "The Full Cost of the Armed Forces in the 370s," above).

120. Quotation from Robbins 1918: 371.

121. For this lifespan, see Blackman 1969: 214–216; Cook 1990: 92–93.

5

1. On this ill-conceived attempt, see Chapter 4.

2. Roisman 2005: 192–195.

3. For the Phaeacians and their ancient reception history, see Dickie 1984.

4. For the return of fleets to this scale by 353/2, see Burckhardt 1995: 114; Cawkwell 1962a: 130, 139 and 1984: 334–335. For six months as an average length of service in the 360s, see Chapter 4.

5. Raaflaub writes (2001: 319–320): "Foreign policy and wars provided the bulk of the assembly's agenda and most of the contentious issues. This was the sphere in which politicians could distinguish themselves and here they fought their rhetorical battles. In such an atmosphere proposals for activist and aggressive policies a priori had a better chance: glory and a great reputation for leadership depended on success in action and victory, not on caution, quietism, and peace."

6. Russell 1973: 31–34.

7. On this view, see Chapter 1.

8. Pritchard 2010: 33–36; Yoshitake 2010.

9. Hunt 2010b: 123–131; Pritchard 2010: 38–39.

10. Hunt 2010a: 230 and 2010b: 279–282.

11. E.g., Aeschin. 1.11; Ar. *Ach.* 595–597; Eur. *Supp.* 886–887; Lys. 16.14; Soph. *Aj.* 410; cf. Ar. *Eq.* 943–944.

12. E.g., Ar. *Ach.* 672–685; Eur. *Heracl.* 309–328, 1030–1037, *Supp.* 576–577, and fr. 364 Collard, Cropp, and Lee; Lys. 2.55; Thuc. 2.36.2, 2.62.3; Mills 2010: 164, 166.

13. Raaflaub 2001.

14. Bowden 2005: 10; Hunt 2010b: 268. For this questioning of violence in today's democracies, see Keane 2004 and 2010: 379–388.

15. Hunt 2010b: 250; Low 2010: 357; Pritchard 2010: 40–41, 43.

16. Hunt 2010b: 240–250.

17. Pritchard 1999a: 218–223.

18. Raaflaub 2001: 341.

19. For Aristophanes' and Euripides' treatments of *polemos*, see respectively Konstan 2010 and Mills 2010.

20. Pritchard 2010: 41–43.

21. Blanshard 2010.

22. Hansen 1991: 133; Raaflaub 2001: 319.

23. Hunt 2010b: 11–12.

24. Chapter 4.

25. Pritchard 2010: 6.

26. E.g., Aesch. *Sept.* 10–20, cf. 415–416; Eur. *Heracl.* 824–827; Thuc. 1.144.4, 2.41.5, 2.43.1.

27. Pritchard 2010: 21–27.

28. Akrigg 2007: 29–33; Hansen 1988: 14–28.

WORKS CITED

Akrigg, B. 2007. "The nature and implications of Athens' changed social structure and economy," in *Debating the Athenian Cultural Revolution: Art, Literature, Philosophy, and Politics 430-380 BC*, edited by R. Osborne. Cambridge: 27-43.

Aleshire, S. B. 1994. "Towards a definition of 'state cult' for ancient Athens," in *Ancient Greek Cult Practice from the Epigraphic Evidence*, edited by R. Hägg. Stockholm: 9-16.

Amit, M. 1965. *Athens and the Sea: A Study in Athenian Sea-Power*. Brussels.

Austin, M. M. 1994. "Economy and society," in *The Cambridge Ancient History: Volume IV: The Fourth Century*, second edition, edited by D. M. Lewis, J. Boardman, S. Hornblower, and M. Ostwald. Cambridge: 527-564.

Austin, M. M., and P. Vidal-Naquet. 1977. *Economic and Social History of Ancient Greece: An Introduction*, translated and revised by M. M. Austin. Berkeley, CA.

Badian, E. 2000. "The road to prominence," in *Demosthenes: Statesman and Orator*, edited by I. Worthington. London: 9-44.

Balcer, J. M. 1976, "Imperial magistrates in the Athenian Empire," *Historia* 25: 257-287.

Baldry, H. 1971. *The Greek Tragic Theatre*. London.

Balot, R. K. 2006. *Greek Political Thought*. Malden.

———. 2010. "Democratizing courage in classical Athens," in *War, Democracy and Culture in Classical Athens*, edited by D. M. Pritchard. Cambridge: 88-108.

Barringer, J. M. 2001. *The Hunt in Ancient Greece*. Baltimore, MD.

Bentz, M. 1998. *Panathenäische Preisamphoren: Eine athenische Vasengattung und ihre Funktion vom 6.-4. Jahrhundert v. Chr.* Basel.

———. 2007. "Torch race and vase-painting," in *The Panathenaic Games:*

Proceedings of an International Conference Held at the University of Athens, May 11-12, 2004, edited by O. Palagia and A. Choremi-Spetsieri. Oxford: 73–80.

Blackman, D. 1969. "The Athenian navy and allied naval contributions in the Pentecontaetia," *GRBS* 10: 179–216.

Blamire, A. 2001. "Athenian finance, 454-404 BC," *Hesperia* 70: 99–126.

Blanshard, A. J. L. 2010. "War in the law-court: Some Athenian discussions," in *War, Democracy and Culture in Classical Athens,* edited by D. M. Pritchard. Cambridge: 203–224.

Böckh, A. 1817. *Die Staatshaushaltung der Athener.* Berlin.

———. 1828. *The Public Economy of Athens,* translated by G. C. Lewis, first English edition, 2 volumes. London.

———. 1840. *Urkunden über das Seewesen des attischen Staates.* Berlin.

Boedeker, D., and K. A. Raaflaub. 1998. "Reflections and conclusions: Democracy, empire and the arts in fifth-century Athens," in *Democracy, Empire, and the Arts in Fifth-Century Athens,* edited by D. Boedeker and K. A. Raaflaub. Cambridge, MA: 319–344.

Boersma, J. S. 1970. *Athenian Building Policy from 561/0 to 405/4 BC.* Groningen.

Bowden, H. 2005. *Classical Athens and the Delphic Oracle: Divination and Democracy.* Cambridge.

Braun, K. 1970. "Der Dipylon-Brunnen B1, die Funde," *MDAI(A)* 85: 129–269.

Bremer, J. M. 1993. "Aristophanes on his own poetry," in *Aristophanes,* edited by J. M. Bremer and E. W. Handley. Geneva: 125–165.

Brock, L., A. Geis, and H. Müller. 2006. "The case for a new research agenda: Explaining democratic wars," in *Democratic Wars: Looking at the Dark Side of Democratic Peace,* edited by A. Geis, L. Brock and H. Müller. New York: 195–214.

Brock, R., and S. Hodkinson. 2000. "Introduction: Alternatives to the democratic *polis,*" in *Alternatives to Athens: Varieties of Political Organization in Ancient Greece,* edited by R. Brock and S. Hodkinson. Oxford: 1–43.

Bruit Zaidman, L., and P. Schmitt Pantel. 1992. *Religion in the Greek City,* translated by P. Cartledge. Cambridge.

Brun, P. 1983. *Eisphora—Syntaxis—Stratiotika: Recherches sur les finances militaires d'Athènes au IVe siècle av. J.-C.* Besançon.

Bugh, G. R. 1988. *The Horsemen of Athens.* Princeton.

Burckhardt, L. A. 1995. "Söldner und Bürger als Soldaten für Athen," in *Die athenische Demokratie im. 4. Jahrhundert v. Chr.: Vollendung oder Verfall einer Verfassungsform?: Akten eines Symposiums 3.-7. August 1992, Bellagio,* edited by W. Eder. Stuttgart: 107–133.

————. 1996. *Bürger und Soldaten: Aspekte der politischen und militärischen Rolle athenischer Bürger im Kriegswesen des 4. Jahrhunderts v. Chr.* Stuttgart.

Burian, P. 1997. "Myth into *muthos*: The shaping of tragic plot," in *The Cambridge Companion to Greek Tragedy*, edited by P. E. Easterling. Cambridge: 178–210.

Burke, E. M. 2005. "The habit of subsidization in classical Athens: Toward a thetic ideology," *C&M* 56: 5–47.

Camp, J. M. 1986. *The Athenian Agora: Excavations in the Heart of Classical Athens*. London.

————. 2001. *The Archaeology of Athens*. London.

Cargill, J. 1981. *The Second Athenian League: Empire or Free Alliance?* Berkeley, CA.

Cartledge, P. 1982. Review of Gabrielsen 1981, *Hermathena* 140: 67–69.

Cawkwell, G. L. 1962a. "The defence of Olynthus," *CQ* 12: 122–140.

————. 1962b. "Demosthenes and the stratiotic fund," *Mnemosyne* 15: 377–383.

————. 1963. "Eubulus," *JHS* 83: 47–67.

————. 1983. Review of Gabrielsen 1981, *English Historical Review* 97: 839.

————. 1984. "Athenian naval power in the fourth century," *CQ* 34: 334–345.

Ceccarelli, P. 2004. "Dancing the *pyrrhichē* in Athens," in *Music and the Muses: The Culture of 'Mousikē' in the Classical Athenian City*, edited by P. Murray and P. Wilson. Oxford: 91–117.

Christ, M. R. 1990. "Liturgy avoidance and *antidosis* in classical Athens," *TAPhA* 120: 147–169.

————. 2006. *The Bad Citizen in Classical Athens*. Cambridge.

Clinton, K. 1979. "*IG* i² 5, the Eleusinia, and the Eleusinians," *AJPh* 100: 1–12.

————. 2005. *Eleusis: The Inscriptions on Stone: Documents of the Sanctuary of the Two Goddesses and Public Documents of the Deme: Volume 1A: Text*, Athens.

————. 2008. *Eleusis: The Inscriptions on Stone: Documents of the Sanctuary of the Two Goddesses and Public Documents of the Deme: Volume 2: Commentary*, Athens.

————. 2009. "The Eleusinian Sanctuary during the Peloponnesian War," in *Art in Athens during the Peloponnesian War*, edited by O. Palagia. Cambridge: 52–65.

Coale, A. J., and P. Demeny. 1966. *Regional Model Life Tables and Stable Populations*. Princeton, NJ.

Cook, M. L. 1990. "Timokrates' 50 talents and the cost of ancient warfare," *Eranos* 88: 69–97.

Crowther, N. B. 1985. "Male 'beauty' contests in Greece: The *euandria* and *euexia*," *AC* 54: 285–291.

Csapo, E. 2007. "The men who built the theatres: *Theatropolai, theatronai*, and *arkhitektones*," in *The Greek Theatre and Festivals: Documentary Studies*, edited by P. Wilson. Oxford: 97–121.

Csapo, E., and W. J. Slater. 1994. *The Context of Ancient Drama*. Ann Arbor, MI.

Currie, B. 2005. *Pindar and the Cult of the Heroes*. Oxford.

Davies, J. K. 1967. "Demosthenes on liturgies: A note," *JHS* 87: 33–40.

———. 1971. *Athenian Propertied Families 600–300 B.C.* Oxford.

———. 1978. *Democracy and Classical Greece*. Glasgow.

———. 2004. "Athenian fiscal expertise and its influence." *MediterrAnt* 7: 491–512.

Davison, J. A. 1958. "Notes on the Panathenaea," *JHS* 78: 23–42.

Dawson, S. E. 1995. "Rousseau and Athens in the democratic imagination," *Political Theory Newsletter* 7: 1–6.

De Polignac, F. 1995. *Cults, Territory and the Origins of the Greek City-State*, translated by J. Lloyd. Chicago.

De Ste. Croix, G. E. M. 1975. "Political pay outside Athens," *CQ* 25: 48–52.

———. 1981. *The Class Struggle in the Ancient Greek World from the Archaic Age to the Arab Conquests*. London.

Despotopoulos, C. 1996. "Démocratie et culture," in *Colloque internationale: Démocratie athénienne et culture: Organisé par l'Académie d'Athènes en coopération avec L'UNESCO (23, 24 et 25 novembre 1992)*, edited by M. Sakellariou. Athens: 91–96.

Develin, R. 1984. "From Panathenaia to Panathenaia," *ZPE* 57: 133–138.

Dickie, M. 1984. "Phaeacian athletics," in *Papers of the Liverpool Latin Seminar, Fourth Volume, 1983*, edited by F. Cairns. Liverpool: 237–276.

Dinsmoor, W. B. 1937. "The final account of the Athena Parthenos," *AEph* Part 2: 507–511.

Dover, K. J. 1974. *Greek Popular Morality in the Time of Plato and Aristotle*. Oxford.

Ehrenberg, V. 1951. *The People of Aristophanes*, second edition. Oxford.

Figueira, T. J. 1998. *The Power of Money: Coinage and Politics in the Athenian Empire*. Philadelphia, PA.

Finley, M. I. 1973a. *Democracy Ancient and Modern*. London.

———. 1973b. *The Ancient Economy*. London.

———. 1978. "The fifth-century Athenian empire: A balance-sheet," in *Imperialism in the Ancient World*, edited by P. D. A. Garnsey and C. R. Whittaker. Oxford: 103–126, 306–310.

————. 1983. *Politics in the Ancient World*. Cambridge.

Fisher, N. R. E. 1993. *Slavery in Classical Greece*. London.

————. 2011. "Competitive delights: The social effects of the expanded programme of contests in post-Kleisthenic Athens," in *Competition in the Ancient World*, edited by N. Fisher and H. van Wees. Swansea: 175–219.

Fornara, C. W., and L. J. Samons. 1991. *Athens from Cleisthenes to Pericles*. Berkeley, CA.

Frederiksen, R. 2011. *Greek City Walls of the Archaic Period: 900–480 B.C.* Oxford.

French, A. 1964. *The Growth of the Athenian Economy*. London.

Friend, J. L. 2009. "The Athenian Ephebeia in the Lycurgan Period: 334/3–322/1 B.C." PhD dissertation, The University of Texas at Austin (Austin).

Fröhlich, P. 2000. "Remarques sur la reddition des comptes des stratèges athéniens," *Dike* 3: 81–111.

Gabrielsen, V. 1981. *Remuneration of State Officials in Fourth Century B.C. Athens*. Odense.

————. 1994. *Financing the Athenian Fleet: Public Taxation and Social Relations*. Baltimore, MD.

————. 2007. "Warfare and the state," in *The Cambridge History of Greek and Roman Warfare: Volume I: Greece, the Hellenistic World and the Rise of Rome*, edited by P. Sabin, H. van Wees, and M. Whitby. Cambridge: 248–272.

————. 2008. "Die Kosten der athenischen Flotte in klassischer Zeit," in *Kriegskosten und Kriegsfinanzierung in der Antike*, edited by F. Burrer and H. Müller. Darmstadt: 46–73.

————. 2013. "Finance and taxes," in *A Companion to Ancient Greek Government*, edited by H. Beck. Chichester: 332–348.

Garlan, Y. 1975. *War in the Ancient World: A Social History*, translated by J. Lloyd. London.

————. 1995. "War and peace," in *The Greeks*, edited by J.-P. Vernant, translated by C. Lambert and T. L. Fagan. Chicago: 53–85.

Gauthier, P. 1976. *Un commentaire historique des Poroi de Xénophon*. Geneva.

————. 1993. "Sur l'institution du *misthos* de l'assemblée à Athènes (*Ath. Pol.* 41.3)," in *Aristote et Athènes*, edited by M. Piérart. Fribourg: 231–250.

Goette, H. R. 2007. "'Choregic' or victory monuments of the tribal Panathenaic contests," in *The Panathenaic Games: Proceedings of an International Conference Held at the University of Athens, May 11–12, 2004*, edited by O. Palagia and A. Choremi-Spetsieri. Oxford: 117–126.

Golden, M. 1998. *Sport and Society in Ancient Greece*. Cambridge.

————. 2000. "A decade of demography: Recent trends in the study of Greek and Roman populations," in *Polis and Politics: Studies in Ancient Greek History: Presented to Mogens Herman Hansen on His Sixtieth Birthday, August 20, 2000,* edited by P. Flensted-Jensen, T. H. Nielsen, and L. Rubinstein. Aarhus: 23–40.

Gomme, A. W. 1956. *A Historical Commentary on Thucydides,* 2 volumes. Oxford.

Gomme, A. W., A. Andrewes, and K. J. Dover. 1981. *A Historical Commentary on Thucydides: Volume V: Book VIII.* Oxford.

Hall, E. 2006. *The Theatrical Cast of Athens: Interaction between Ancient Drama and Society.* Oxford.

———. 2007. "Greek tragedy 430–380 BC," in *Debating the Athenian Cultural Revolution: Art, Literature, Philosophy, and Politics 430–380 BC,* edited by R. Osborne. Cambridge: 264–287.

Hamel, D. 1998. *Athenian Generals: Military Authority in the Classical Period.* Boston.

Hansen, M. H. 1976. "How many Athenians attended the *ecclesia*?" *GRBS* 17: 115–134.

———. 1979a. "How often did the Athenian *dicasteria* meet?" *GRBS* 20: 243–246.

———. 1979b. "*Misthos* for magistrates in classical Athens," *SO* 44: 5–22.

———. 1980a. "Perquisites for magistrates in fourth-century Athens," *C&M* 32: 105–125.

———. 1980b. "Seven hundred *archai* in classical Athens," *GRBS* 21: 151–173.

———. 1983. "The Athenian politicians, 403–322 BC," *GRBS* 24: 35–55.

———. 1986a. *Demography and Democracy: The Number of Athenian Citizens in the Fourth Century B.C.* Herning.

———. 1986b. "The construction of Pnyx II and the introduction of assembly pay," *C&M* 37: 89–98.

———. 1987. *The Athenian Assembly in the Age of Demosthenes.* Oxford.

———. 1988. *Three Studies in Athenian Demography.* Copenhagen.

———. 1991. *The Athenian Democracy in the Age of Demosthenes: Structure, Principles and Ideology,* translated by J. A. Crook. Cambridge, MA.

———. 2006a. *Polis: An Introduction to the Ancient Greek City-State.* Oxford.

———. 2006b. *Studies in the Population of Aigina, Athens and Eretria.* Copenhagen.

———. 2006c. *The Shotgun Method: The Demography of the Ancient Greek City-State Culture.* Columbia, MO.

Hansen, M. H., and T. H. Nielsen. 2004. *An Inventory of Archaic and Classical Poleis.* Oxford.

Hanson, V. D. 1998. *Warfare and Agriculture in Classical Greece*, revised edition. Berkeley, CA.

———. 2000. "Hoplite battle as ancient Greek warfare: When, where, and why?" in *War and Violence in Ancient Greece*, edited by H. van Wees. London: 201–232.

Harding, P. 1988. "Athenian defensive strategy in the fourth century," *Phoenix* 42: 61–71.

———. 1995. "Athenian foreign policy in the fourth century," *Klio* 77: 105–125.

Harris, D. 1995. *The Treasures of the Parthenon and Erechtheion*. Oxford.

Harris, E. M. 2000. "Open texture in Athenian law," *Dike* 3: 27–79.

———. 2006. *Democracy and the Rule of Law in Classical Athens: Essays on Law, Society and Politics*. Cambridge.

———. 2010. "The rule of law and military organisation in the Greek *poleis*," in *Symposion 2009: Vorträge zur griechischen und hellenistischen Rechtsgeschichte (Seggau, 25.-30. August 2009)*, edited by G. Thür. Vienna: 405–415.

———. 2013. *The Rule of Law in Action in Democratic Athens*. Oxford.

Harrison, A. R. W. 1971. *The Law of Athens: Procedure*. Oxford.

Healey, R. F. 1990. *Eleusinian Sacrifices in the Athenian Law Code*. New York.

Hedrick, C. W. 1999. "Democracy and the Athenian epigraphic habit," *Hesperia* 68: 387–439.

Henry, A. S. 1983. *Honours and Privileges in Athenian Decrees: The Principal Formulae of Athenian Honorary Decrees*. Hildesheim.

Heskel, J. 1997. *The North Aegean Wars, 371-360 B.C.* Stuttgart.

Hignett, C. 1952. *A History of the Athenian Constitution to the End of the Fifth Century B.C.* Oxford.

Hodkinson, S. 1999. "An agonistic society? Athletic competition in archaic and classical Spartan society," in *Sparta: New Perspectives*, edited by S. Hodkinson and A. Powell. London: 147–187.

Hornblower, S. 1991. *A Commentary on Thucydides*, Volume 1. Oxford.

———. 2002. *The Greek World 479-323 BC*, third edition. London.

Humphreys, S. C. 2004. *The Strangeness of Gods: Historical Perspectives on the Interpretation of Athenian Religion*. Oxford.

Hunt, P. 2010a. "Athenian militarism and the recourse to war," in *War, Democracy and Culture in Classical Athens*, edited by D. M. Pritchard. Cambridge: 225–242.

———. 2010b. *War, Peace and Alliance in Demosthenes' Athens*. Cambridge.

Hunter, V. J. 1994. *Policing Athens: Social Control in the Attic Lawsuits, 420-320 B.C.* Princeton, NJ.

Jacob, O. 1928. *Les esclaves publics à Athènes*. Liege and Paris.

Jacquemin, A. 2000. *Guerre et religion dans le monde grec (490–322 av. J.-C.)*. Paris.

Jameson, M. 1980. "Apollo Lykeias at Athens," *Arkhaiognosia* 1: 213–236.

———. 1988. "Sacrifice and animal husbandry in classical Greece," in *Pastoral Economies in Classical Antiquity*, edited by C. R. Whittaker. Cambridge: 87–119.

———. 1999. "The spectacular and the obscure in Athenian religion," in *Performance Culture and Athenian Democracy*, edited by S. Goldhill and R. Osborne. Cambridge: 321–340.

Johnston, A. W. 1987. "*IG* ii² 2311 and the number of Panathenaic amphorae," *ABSA* 82: 125–129.

———. 2007. "Panathenaic amphorae, again," *ZPE* 161: 101–104.

Jones, A. H. M. 1952. "The economic basis of the Athenian democracy," *P&P* 1: 13–31.

———. 1957. *Athenian Democracy*. Oxford.

Jones, C. P. 1987. "*Stigma*: Branding and tattooing in the Graeco-Roman antiquity," *JRS* 77: 139–155.

Kallet, L. 1998. "Accounting for culture in fifth-century Athens," in *Democracy, Empire, and the Arts in Fifth-Century Athens*, edited by D. Boedeker and K. A. Raaflaub. Cambridge, MA: 43–58.

Kallet-Marx, L. 1989. "Did tribute fund the Parthenon?" *ClAnt* 8: 252–266.

———. 1994. "Money talks: *Rhetor, demos* and the resources of the Athenian empire," in *Ritual, Finance, Politics: Athenian Democratic Accounts Presented to David Lewis*, edited by R. Osborne and S. Hornblower. Oxford: 227–251.

Kamen, D. 2013. *Status in Classical Athens*. Princeton, NJ.

Keane, J. C. 2004. *Violence and Democracy*. Cambridge.

———. 2010. "Epilogue: Does Democracy Have a Violent Heart," in *War, Democracy and Culture in Classical Athens*, edited by D. M. Pritchard. Cambridge: 378–408.

Kennedy, G. A. 1985. "Oratory," in *The Cambridge History of Classical Literature: Volume I: Greek Literature*, edited by P. E. Easterling and B. M. W. Knox. Cambridge: 498–526.

Konstan, D. 2010. "Ridiculing a popular war: Old comedy and militarism in classical Athens," in *War, Democracy and Culture in Classical Athens*, edited by D. M. Pritchard. Cambridge: 184–200.

Kroll, J. H. 1977. "An archive of the Athenian cavalry," *Hesperia* 46: 83–140.

Kyle, D. G. 1987. *Athletics in Ancient Athens*. Leiden.

———. 1992. "The Panathenaic games: Sacred and civic athletics," in *Goddess and Polis: The Panathenaic Festival in Ancient Greece*, edited by J. Neils. Hanover, NH: 77–101.

———. 2007. *Sport and Spectacle in the Ancient World*. Malden.

Kyriazis, N. 2012. *Why Ancient Greece? The Birth and Development of Democracy*. Athens.

Lambert, S. D. 2004. "Athenian state laws and decrees, 352/1–322/1: Part I: Decrees honouring Athenians," *ZPE* 150: 85–119.

———. 2005. "Athenian state laws and decrees, 352/1–322/1: Part II: Religious regulations," *ZPE* 153: 125–159.

———. 2012. "Some political shifts in Lykourgan Athens," in *Clisthène et Lycurgue d'Athènes: Autour du politique dans la cité classique*, edited by V. Azoulay and P. Ismard. Paris: 175–190.

Leppin, H. 1992. "Die *arkhontes en tais polesi* des Delisch-Attischen Seebundes," *Historia* 41: 257–271.

Lewis, D. M. 1982. Review of Gabrielsen 1981, *JHS* 102: 269.

———. 1990. "Public property in the city," in *The Greek City: From Homer to Alexander*, edited by O. Murray and S. Price. Oxford: 245–264.

———. 1997. *Selected Papers in Greek and Near Eastern History*, edited by P. J. Rhodes. Cambridge.

Linders, T. 1975. *Treasurers of the Other Gods in Athens and Their Functions*. Meisenheim am Glan.

Lissarrague, F. 1990. *L'autre guerrier: archers, peltastes, cavaliers dans l'imagerie attique*. Paris.

Lonis, R. 1979. *Guerre et religion en Grèce à l'époque classique: Recherches sur les rites, les dieux, l'idéologie de la victoire*. Paris.

Loomis, W. T. 1995. "Pay differentials and class warfare in Lysias' *Against Theozotides*: Two obols or two drachmas," *ZPE* 107: 230–236.

———. 1998. *Wages, Welfare Costs and Inflation in Classical Athens*. Ann Arbor, MI.

Low, P. 2010. "Commemoration of the war dead in classical Athens: Remembering defeat and victory," in *War, Democracy and Culture in Classical Athens*, edited by D. M. Pritchard. Cambridge: 341–358.

MacDowell, D. M. 1983. Review of Gabrielsen 1981, *CR* 33: 75–76.

Mader, G. 2006. "Fighting Philip with decrees: Demosthenes and the syndrome of symbolic action," *AJPh* 127: 376–386.

Mahaffy, J. P. 1892. *Problems in Greek History*, London.

Marr, J. L., and P. J. Rhodes. 2008. *The "Old Oligarch": The Constitution of the Athenians Attributed to Xenophon*. Oxford.

Meiggs, R. 1972. *The Athenian Empire*. Oxford.

Meiggs, R., and D. M. Lewis. 1969. *A Selection of Greek Historical Documents to the End of the Fifth Century B.C.* Oxford.

Meritt, B. D., and J. S. Traill. 1974. *The Athenian Agora XV: Inscriptions: The Athenian Councillors*. Princeton, NJ.

Meritt, B. D., H. T. Wade-Gery, and M. F. McGregor. 1950. *The Athenian Tribute Lists*, Volume 3. Princeton, NJ.

Mikalson, J. D. 1975. *The Sacred and the Civil Calendar of the Athenian Year*. Princeton, NJ.

———. 2005. *Ancient Greek Religion*. Malden.

Miller, S. G. 2003. "The organization and functioning of the Olympic Games," in *Sport and Festival in the Ancient Greek World*, edited by D. J. Phillips and D. Pritchard. Swansea: 1–40.

———. 2004. *Ancient Greek Athletics*. London.

Millett, P. 1993. "War, economy, and democracy in classical Athens," in *War and Society in the Greek World*, edited by J. Rich and G. Shipley. London and New York: 177–196.

———. 2009. "Finance and resources: Public, private and personal," in *A Companion to Ancient History*, edited by A. Erskine. Chichester: 474–485.

Mills, S. 2010. "Affirming Athenian action: Euripides' portrayal of military activity and the limits of tragic instruction," in *War, Democracy and Culture in Classical Athens*, edited by D. M. Pritchard. Cambridge: 163–183.

Milns, R. D. 2000. "The public speeches of Demosthenes," in *Demosthenes: Statesman and Orator*, edited by I. Worthington. New York: 205–223.

Möller, A. 2007. "Classical Greece: Distribution," edited by W. Scheidel, I. Morris, and R. Sallar. Cambridge: 362–384.

Mossé, C. 1962. *La fin de la démocratie athénienne: Aspects sociaux et politiques du déclin de la cité grecque au IVe siècle avant J.-C.* Paris.

Neils, J. 1992a. "The Panathenaia: An introduction," in *Goddess and Polis: The Panathenaic Festival in Ancient Greece*, edited by J. Neils. Hanover, NH: 13–27.

———. 1992b. "Panathenaic amphorae: Their meaning, makers, and markets," in *Goddess and Polis: The Panathenaic Festival in Ancient Greece*, edited by J. Neils. Hanover, NH: 28–51.

Norena, C. F. 2011. "Coins and Communication," in *The Oxford Handbook of Social Relations in the Roman World*, edited by M. Peachin. Oxford: 248–268.

Ober, J. 1978. "Views of sea power in the fourth-century Attic orators," *AncW* 1: 119–130.

———. 1989. *Mass and Elite in Democratic Athens: Rhetoric, Ideology, and the Power of the People*. Princeton, NJ.

———. 1998. *Political Dissent in Democratic Athens*. Princeton, NJ.

———. 2008. *Democracy and Knowledge: Innovation and Learning in Classical Athens*. Princeton, NJ.

———. 2014. "Fiscal policy in classical Athens," in *Fiscal Regimes and the Political Economy of Premodern States*, edited by W. Scheidel and A. Monson. Cambridge.

Osborne, R. G. 1985. *Demos: The Discovery of Classical Attika*. Cambridge.

———. 1987. Review of Hansen 1986, *JHS* 107: 233.

———. 1993. "Competitive festivals and the *polis*: A context for the dramatic festivals at Athens," in *Tragedy, Comedy and the Polis: Papers from the Greek Drama Conference Nottingham 18-20 July 1990*, edited by A. H. Sommerstein et al. Bari: 21–38.

———. 2004. *LACTOR 2: The Old Oligarch: Pseudo-Xenophon's Constitution of the Athenians: Introduction, Translation and Commentary*. London.

———. 2007. "Tracing cultural revolution in classical Athens," in *Debating the Athenian Cultural Revolution: Art, Literature, Philosophy, and Politics 430-380 BC*, edited by R. G. Osborne. Cambridge: 1–26.

Ostwald, M. 1986. *From Popular Sovereignty to the Sovereignty of Law: Law, Society and Politics in Fifth-Century Athens*. Berkeley, CA.

Parker, R. 1987. "Myths of early Athens," in *Interpretations of Greek Mythology*, edited by J. Bremmer. London: 197–214.

———. 1996. *Athenian Religion: A History*. Oxford.

———. 2005. *Polytheism and Society at Athens*. Oxford.

Phillips, D. J. 1981. "Participation in Athenian democracy," *Ancient Society: Resources for Teachers* [the journal is now *AH*] 11: 5–48.

———. 2012. "Athens," in *The Edinburgh Companion to the History of Democracy*, edited by S. Stockwell and B. Isakhan. Edinburgh: 97–108.

Phillips, D. J., and D. Pritchard. 2003. "Introduction," in *Sport and Festival in the Ancient Greek World*, edited by D. J. Phillips and D. Pritchard. Swansea: vii–xxxi.

Pickard-Cambridge, A. 1988. *The Dramatic Festivals of Athens*, second edition, revised by J. Gould and D. M. Lewis with a new supplement. Oxford.

Pinney, G. F. 1988. "Pallas and Panathenaea," in *Proceedings of the 3rd Symposium on Ancient Greek and Related Pottery: Copenhagen August 31-September 4 1987*, edited by J. Christiansen and T. Melander. Copenhagen: 465–477.

Plassart, A. 1913. "Les archers d'Athènes," *REG* 26: 151–213.

Podlecki, A. J. 1998. *Perikles and His Circle*. London.

Pritchard, D. M. 1994. "From hoplite republic to thetic democracy: The social context of the reforms of Ephialtes," *AH* 24: 111–140.

———. 1998. "'The fractured imaginary': Popular thinking on military matters in fifth-century Athens," *AH* 28: 38–61.

———. 1999a. "The Fractured Imaginary: Popular Thinking on Citizen Soldiers and Warfare in Fifth-Century Athens." PhD dissertation, Macquarie University (Sydney).

———. 1999b. "Fool's gold and silver: Reflections on the evidentiary status of finely painted Attic pottery," *Antichthon* 33: 1–27.

———. 2000. "Tribal solidarity and participation in fifth-century Athens: A summary," *AH* 31: 104–118.

———. 2003. "Athletics, education and participation in classical Athens," in *Sport and Festival in the Ancient Greek World*, edited by D. J. Phillips and D. Pritchard. Swansea: 293–349.

———. 2004. "Kleisthenes, participation, and the dithyrambic contests of late archaic and classical Athens," *Phoenix* 58: 208–228.

———. 2005a. "War and democracy in ancient Athens: A Preliminary Report," *Classicum* 31: 16–25.

———. 2005b. "Kleisthenes and Athenian democracy: Vision from above or below?" *Polis* 22: 136–157.

———. 2007a. "Costing the armed forces of Athens during the Peloponnesian War," *AH* 37: 125–135.

———. 2007b. "How do democracy and war affect each other? The case study of ancient Athens," *Polis* 24: 328–352.

———. 2009. "Sport, war and democracy in classical Athens," *The International Journal of the History of Sport* 26.2: 212–245.

———. 2010. "The symbiosis between democracy and war: The case of ancient Athens," in *War, Democracy and Culture in Classical Athens*, edited by D. M. Pritchard. Cambridge: 1–62.

———. 2012a. "Aristophanes and de Ste. Croix: The value of old comedy as evidence for Athenian popular culture," *Antichthon* 45: 14–51.

———. 2012b. "Costing festivals and war: Spending priorities of the Athenian Democracy," *Historia* 61: 18–65.

———. 2013. *Sport, Democracy and War in Classical Athens*. Cambridge.

———. 2014. "The public payment of magistrates in fourth-century Athens," *GRBS* 54: 1–16.

Pritchett, W. K. 1956. "The Attic stelai: Part II," *Hesperia* 25: 178–323.

———. 1961. "Five new fragments of the Attic *stelai*," *Hesperia* 30: 23–29.

———. 1971. *The Greek State at War: Part I*. Berkeley, CA.

———. 1985. *The Greek State at War: Part IV*. Berkeley, CA.

Raaflaub, K. A. 2001. "Father of all, destroyer of all: War in late fifth-century Athenian discourse and ideology," in *War and Democracy: A Comparative Study of the Korean War and the Peloponnesian War*, edited by D. R. McCann and B. S. Strauss. Armonk, NY: 307–356.

———. 2007. "Warfare in Athenian society," in *The Cambridge Companion to the Age of Pericles*, edited by L. J. Samons. Cambridge: 96–124.

Randall, R. J. 1953. "The Erechtheum Workmen," *AJA* 57: 199–210.

Revermann, M. 2006. "The competence of theatre audiences in fifth- and fourth-century Athens," *JHS* 126: 99–124.

Rhodes, P. J. 1972. *The Athenian Boule*. Oxford.

———. 1981. *A Commentary on the Aristotelian Athenaion Politeia*. Oxford.

———. 1988. *Thucydides History II, Edited with Translation and Commentary*. Warminster.

———. 2003. *Ancient Democracy and Modern Ideology*. London.

———. 2006. *A History of the Classical Greek World*. Malden.

———. 2008. "After the three-bar sigma controversy: The history of Athenian imperialism reassessed," *CQ* 58: 500–506.

———. 2009. "State and religion in Athenian inscriptions," *G&R* 56: 1–13.

———. 2013. "The organisation of Athenian public finance," *G&R* 40: 203–231.

Rhodes, P. J., and R. Osborne (eds.). 2003. *Greek Historical Inscriptions 404–323 BC*. Oxford.

Robb, K. 1994. *Literacy and Paideia in Ancient Greece*. New York.

Robbins, F. E. 1918. "The cost to Athens of her second empire," *CPh* 13: 361–388.

Roisman, J. 2005. *The Rhetoric of Manhood: Masculinity in the Attic Orators*. Berkeley, CA.

Roselli, D. K. 2009. "*Theorika* in fifth-century Athens," *GRBS* 49: 5–30.

———. 2011. *Theater of the People: Spectators and Society in Ancient Athens*. Austin, TX.

Rosivach, V. J. 1985 (1992). "Manning the Athenian fleet, 433–426 BC," *AJAH* 10: 41–66.

———. 1994. *The System of Public Sacrifice in Fourth-Century Athens*. Atlanta, GA.

———. 2001. "Class matters in the *Dyskolos* of Menander," *CQ* 51: 127–134.

———. 2010. "*IG* i³ 82 and the date of the introduction of bouleutic *misthos* in Athens," *ZPE* 175: 145–149.

———. 2011. "State pay as war relief in Peloponnesian-War Athens," *G&R* 58: 176–183.

Ruschenbusch, E. 1979. "Die Einführung des Theorikon," *ZPE* 36: 303–308.

Russell, D. A. 1973. *Plutarch*. London.

Samons, L. J. 2000. *Empire of the Owl: Athenian Imperial Finance*. Stuttgart.

———. 2001. "Democracy, empire, and the search for the Athenian character," *Arion*, third series, 8.3: 128–157.

———. 2004. *What's Wrong with Democracy? From Athenian Practice to American Worship*. Berkeley, CA.

Sandys, J. E. 1897. *The First Philippic and the Olynthiacs of Demosthenes with Introduction and Critical and Explanatory Notes*. London.

———. 1910. *A History of Classical Scholarship: Volume 3: The Eighteenth Century in Germany, and the Nineteenth Century in Europe and the United States of America*. London.

Scanlon, T. E. 1983. "The vocabulary of competitions: *Agon* and *aethlos*: Greek terms for contest," *Arete* 1: 147–162.

———. 1988. "Combat and contest: Athletic metaphors for warfare in Greek literature," in *Coroebus Triumphs: The Alliance of Sport and the Arts*, edited by S. J. Bandy. San Diego, CA: 230–244.

———. 2002. *Eros and Greek Athletics*. Oxford.

Seaford, R. 1984. *Euripides Cyclops with Introduction and Commentary*. Oxford.

Shear, J. L. 2001. "Polis and Panathenaia: The History and Development of Athena's Festival." PhD dissertation, University of Pennsylvania (Philadelphia).

———. 2003a. "Prizes from Athens: The list of Panathenaic prizes and the sacred oil," *ZPE* 142: 87–105.

———. 2003b. "Atarbos' base and the Panathenaia," *JHS* 123: 164–180.

Simms, R. M. 1975. "The Eleusinia in the sixth to fourth centuries B.C.," *GRBS* 16: 269–279.

Sinclair, R. K. 1978. "The King's Peace and the employment of military and naval forces 387–378," *Chiron* 8: 30–54.

———. 1988. *Democracy and Participation in Athens*. Cambridge.

Slater, W. 2007. "Deconstructing festivals," in *The Greek Theatre and Festivals: Documentary Studies*, edited by P. Wilson. Oxford: 21–47.

Sommerstein, A. H. 1981. *Aristophanes* Knights, *Edited with Translation and Notes*. Warminster.

———. 1983. *Aristophanes* Wasps, *Edited with Translation and Notes*. Warminster.

———. 1987. *Aristophanes* Birds, *Edited with Translation and Notes*. Warminster.

———. 1997. A response to Slater 1997, in *Education in Greek Fiction*, edited by A. H. Sommerstein and C. Atherton. Bari: 53–64.

———. 1998. *Aristophanes* Wealth, *Edited with Translation and Notes.* Warminster.

Sourvinou-Inwood, C. 1990. "What is *polis* religion?" in *The Greek City: From Homer to Alexander,* edited by O. Murray and S. Price. Oxford: 295–322.

Spence, I. G. 1993. *The Cavalry of Classical Greece: A Social and Military History with Particular Reference to Athens.* Oxford.

———. 2010. "Cavalry, democracy and military thinking in classical Athens," in *War, Democracy and Culture in Classical Athens,* edited by D. M. Pritchard. Cambridge: 111–138.

Stanier, R. S. 1953. "The cost of the Parthenon," *JHS* 73: 68–76.

Stevenson, T. 2003. "The Parthenon frieze as an idealized, contemporary Panathenaic festival," in *Sport and Festival in the Ancient Greek World,* edited by D. J. Phillips and D. Pritchard. Swansea: 233–280.

Stockton, D. 1990. *The Classical Athenian Democracy.* New York.

Stroud, R. S. 1971. "Theozotides and the Athenian orphans," *Hesperia* 40: 280–301.

———. 1974. "An Athenian law on silver coinage," *Hesperia* 43: 157–188.

———. 1982. Review of Gabrielsen 1981, *AHR* 78: 158–159.

Taylor, C. 2001a. "Bribery in Athenian politics part I: Accusations, allegations and slander," *G&R* 48: 53–66.

———. 2001b. "Bribery in Athenian politics part II: Ancient reaction and reception," *G&R* 48: 154–172.

Themelis, P. 2007. "Panathenaic prizes and dedications," in *The Panathenaic Games: Proceedings of an International Conference Held at the University of Athens, May 11–12, 2004,* edited by O. Palagia and A. Choremi-Spetsieri. Oxford: 53–58.

Thomas, R. 2009. "Writing, reading, public and private 'literacies,'" in *Ancient Literacies: The Culture of Reading in Greece and Rome,* edited by W. A. Johnson and H. N. Parker. Oxford: 13–45.

Todd, S. C. 1993. *The Shape of Athenian Law.* Oxford.

Tracy, S. V. 2007. "Games at the Lesser Panathenaia?" in *The Panathenaic Games: Proceedings of an International Conference Held at the University of Athens, May 11–12, 2004,* edited by O. Palagia and A. Choremi-Spetsieri. Oxford: 53–58.

Traill, J. S. 1969. "The *bouleutai* list of 281/0 B.C.," *Hesperia* 38: 459–494.

Trundle, M. 2010. "Light troops in classical Athens," in *War, Democracy and Culture in Classical Athens,* edited by D. M. Pritchard. Cambridge: 139–160.

Unz, R. K. 1985. "The surplus of the Athenian *phoros,*" *GRBS* 26: 21–42.

Valavanis, P. 1986. "Les amphores panathénaïques et le commerce athénien de l'huile," in *Recherches sur les amphores grecques*, edited by J.-Y. Empereur and Y. Garlan. Paris: 453–460.

———. 1997. "*Bakkhios, Kittos kai panathēnaikaoi amphoreis: Skepseis gia tē domē tōn attikōn keramikōn ergastēriōn tou 4ou ai. p.Kh*," in *Athenian Potters and Painters: The Conference Proceedings*, edited by J. H. Oakley, W. D. E. Coulson, and O. Palagia. Oxford: 85–95.

Van Wees, H. 2000. "The city at war," in *Classical Greece 500-323 BC*, edited by R. Osborne. Oxford: 81–110.

———. 2004. *Greek Warfare: Myths and Realities*. London.

Vanderpool, E. 1942. "An archaic inscribed stele from Marathon," *Hesperia* 2: 329–337.

———. 1969. "Three prize vases," *AD* 24: 1–5, Plates 1–4.

Vickers, M., and D. Gill. 1994. *Artful Crafts: Ancient Greek Silverware and Pottery*. Oxford.

Wallace, R. W. 1997. "Poet, public and 'theatrocracy': Audience performance in classical Athens," in *Poet, Public, and Performance in Ancient Greece*, edited by L. Edmunds and R. W. Wallace. Baltimore, MD: 97–111.

Walters, H. B. 1891. "The newly-discovered treatise of Aristotle," *CR* 5: 69–72.

Walton, M. 1977. "Financial arrangements for the Athenian dramatic festivals," *Theatre Research International* 2: 79–86.

West, A. B. 1930. "Cleon's assessment and the Athenian budget," *TAPAh* 61: 217–239.

Wilson, C. H. 1970. "Athenian military finances, 378/7 to the peace of 375," *Athenaeum* 48: 302–326.

Wilson, P. 2000. *The Athenian Institution of the Khoregia: The Chorus, the City and the Stage*. Cambridge.

———. 2003. "The politics of dance: Dithyrambic contest and social order in ancient Greece," in *Sport and Festival in the Ancient Greek World*, edited by D. J. Phillips and D. Pritchard. Swansea: 163–196.

———. 2007. "Choruses for sale in Thorikos? A speculative note on *SEG* 34, 107," *ZPE* 161: 125–132.

———. 2008. "Costing the Dionysia," in *Performance, Reception, Iconography: Studies in Honour of Oliver Taplin*, edited by M. Revermann and P. Wilson. Oxford: 88–127.

———. 2009. "Tragic honours and democracy: Neglected evidence for the politics of the Athenian Dionysia," *CQ* 59: 9–29.

Winkler, J. J. 1990. "The ephebes' song: *Tragōidia* and *polis*," in *Nothing to Do with Dionysos? Athenian Drama in Its Social Context*, edited by J. J. Winkler and F. I. Zeitlin. Princeton, NJ: 20–62.

Winkler, J. J., and F. I. Zeitlin (eds.). 1990. *Nothing to Do with Dionysos? Athenian Drama in Its Social Context*. Princeton, NJ.

Wood, E. M. 1988. *Peasant-Citizen and Slave: The Foundations of Athenian Democracy*. London.

Woodford, S. 1971. "Cults of Heracles in Attica," in *Studies Presented to George M. A. Hanfmann*, edited by D. G. Mitten, J. D. Pedley, and J. A. Scott. Mainz: 211–225.

Yakobson, A. 2011. "Political stability and public order: Athens vs. Rome," in *Stability and Crisis in the Athenian Democracy*, edited by G. Herman. Stuttgart: 139–156.

Yoshitake, S. 2010. "*Aretē* and the achievements of the war dead: The logic of praise in the Athenian funeral oration," in *War, Democracy and Culture in Classical Athens*, edited by D. M. Pritchard. Cambridge: 359–377.

Young, D. C. 1984. *The Olympic Myth of Greek Amateur Athletics*. Chicago.

Zimmermann, B. 1996. "Das Lied der Polis: Zur Geschichte des Dithyrambos," in *Tragedy, Comedy and the Polis: Papers from the Greek Drama Conference Nottingham, 18-20 July 1990*, edited by A. H. Sommerstein, S. Halliwell, J. Henderson, and B. Zimmermann. Bari: 39–54.

INDEX OF SOURCES

GENERAL INDEX